HELENE THORNTON

BIG GIRLS DON'T CRY

THE WILD AND WICKED WORLD OF PAULA YATES' MOTHER

JOHN BLAKE

Published by John Blake Publishing Ltd,
3, Bramber Court, 2 Bramber Road,
London W14 9PB, England

www.blake.co.uk

First published in hardback in 2006

ISBN 1 84454 252 1

British Library Cataloguing-in-Publication Data:

A catalogue record for this book is available from the British Library

Design by www.envydesign.co.uk

Printed in Great Britain by Creative, Print & Design

1 3 5 7 9 10 8 6 4 2

Papers used by John Blake Publishing are natural, recyclable products
made from wood grown in sustainable forests. The manufacturing processes
conform to the environmental regulations of the country of origin.

Every attempt has been made to contact the relevant copyright-holders,
but some were unobtainable. We would be grateful if the appropriate people
could contact us.

Dedication

I dedicate this book to Bob Geldof, the best son-in-law in the world, who taught me when attacked by those who don't know me to 'keep your head down Helene'. I did and I thank him for the advice and for his kindness over the decades of our relationship. A great gentleman and a lovely man.

I would like to thank my cousin, Diane Laugharne, for her support over half a century. I told her when she was six weeks old and in her cot that I needed a sister and if she wanted she could be my chosen one. She must have understood, because she's been a truly loyal 'sister'.

PREFACE

The winter sky was grey, the cold intense. A swirling mist edged over centuries old yews, obscuring the distant view. The silence was eerie. I was three and a half years old and afraid in this strange home of an army of phantoms.

Looking up at my mother, I wondered why lately she kept visiting the cemetery. No one in our family had died. Why did she bring me here? Gertrude's face was ashen, her thin lips tight and she stared at me, unseeing, with her near-black, eagle's eyes. I wished we could go to the market and look at the flower stalls,or to the beach to watch the tide come in. I loved watching the sea.

Then, suddenly, Gertrude stopped in front of a big, square, dark hole in the ground and, turning to me, said,

'That's the hole where they'll put someone dead in his coffin. It's dark and deep, isn't it? Someday, I'll put you in one of those holes and then I'll cover you with soil so you can never get out.'

God must have been with me that day, because as I looked into my mother's face and saw the sadistic excitement in her eyes I knew by some primitive instinct that I must show no fear, nothing of my feelings of horror, terror and pitiful confusion. Disappointed, Gertrude marched on and we returned home. I never forgot what had happened and today, over sixty years later, the image is as clear as ever.

To love a human being who is mentally unstable is a tragedy. It happened to me three times in my life. Those three people caused havoc in the lives of everyone who loved them. On the positive side, a traumatic childhood made me resilient, capable of passing through the fires of hell and anguish and continuing on to the end of my particular road. What follows is true, written, in all humility, to tell my story and to set the record straight for the grandchildren I love – Fifi, Peaches and Pixie Geldof and Miss Tiger Hutchence.

CONTENTS

PART ONE: ELAINE

PART TWO: THE MARRIED YEARS – JESS YATES' MARIONETTE

PART THREE: GLIMPSES OF FRIENDS, ENEMIES, PLACES AND TRAINS

PART FOUR: THE GIRL WITH BLUE GLASS EYES

PART ONE

ELAINE

'And I come to the fields and
vast palaces of memory...'

SAINT AUGUSTIN, 354-430AD, *CONFESSIONS*, BOOK X

CHAPTER ONE

Once, in the middle of the night, I woke and lay listening to a plane droning overhead. The engine had a curious throb, so it was a German plane – my grandad, George, had taught me that. I was four years old and always curious, so despite my fear of the 'enemy', I rose, crept to the window and lifted the blackout curtain to see if I could spot the plane. Instead, I saw something I have never forgotten, a yellowish-orange sky in the middle of the night. I was so astonished, I ran to my mother's bedroom and woke her.

'The sky is orange! Why is it orange in the middle of the night?'

She replied, 'It's orange because Liverpool is burning. Now please go to sleep.'

Returning to my room, I lay in the darkness thinking of Liverpool burning. It wasn't far from our town, Blackpool, and my nana, Constance, had told me that Liverpudlians were very brave people. I thought of the children and the houses falling in ruins under the bombs. Then I pulled the bedclothes over my head and tried to sleep, despite the noise of bombs being unloaded not far away as our planes pursued the Germans from Liverpool.

We always slept in the house as Gertrude, my mother, wouldn't go into the nearby air raid shelter because someone had told her there was a frog in residence there, despite what my father, Bill, said. She had phobias of dogs, cats, frogs, toads and anything that could run faster than she could. I was taught from the beginning that all dogs and cats bit people who approached them and that I had to cross the road to avoid contact with such animals. I therefore crossed a number of dangerous roads to avoid being eaten by a cat, dog, dinosaur, even the neighbour's parrot.

My nana had told me that the Germans couldn't bomb our town because they would get the wings of their planes caught in the girders of the Blackpool Tower. I believed this, because Nana had said it and I was comforted by the thought, but often I lay awake, thinking of the orange-yellow sky outside and Liverpool burning. Not sleeping when worried was to be a leitmotif of my life.

I was a shy child, intelligent and sensitive to people's moods. My principal quality was generosity; my great fault was a tendency to laugh like a gong when I shouldn't. If an

Olympic gold for giggling had existed, I would have won it hands down. What I liked best was being at home, lying in the long grass of my father's allotment, watching bees and smelling the clover flowers. I was born a recluse and when invited to a children's party would often return home after a few minutes, having handed over a gift and been polite to the parents. When visitors arrived in the house, I had the bad habit of hiding under the table, concealed from view by the long tablecloth that touched the floor. I made the mistake of doing this once at Nana's house and came close to giving her a heart attack. At an interesting point in the conversation, I suddenly chimed in. Nana, who had not realised I was under the table, turned pale and when she had recovered marched me off to my mother. She said that it was time to rid me of my shyness and suggested that I be auditioned for the Tiny Tots of the Blackpool Children's Pantomime, held each year at the Grand Theatre.

Teeth chattering with terror, I was taken to audition and sang a scale for the producer. To my horror, I was accepted and rehearsals began. This pleased my mother, because she was stage-struck. I wasn't and wondered what it was all about. I soon found out.

When the Tiny Tots lined up on opening night to perform the song 'In an Eighteenth-Century Square', I was there and ready to sing, as we had at rehearsals. Then the curtain rose, and for the first time, I saw a packed theatre with hundreds of faces looking at us, spotlights that dazzled and the conductor all dressed up in his evening clothes. Panic hit me and I took a tiny step sideways towards the wings. I was about to take a second step towards freedom, when I saw my mum glowering at me from the wings, and, scared, I took a small step back. It was an unpromising start to Nana's bid to give me more self-confidence, but eventually it succeeded. I did a number of shows over the next eight years, learning to enter and leave a stage and take my bow.

Life during the war seemed unreal. On the one hand, food shortages left everyone hungry, but on the other, there was a sense of national unity and deep patriotism rarely seen in normal times. Due to her difficult nature, my mother was often furious with my father, so I used to walk alone to the sea and watch the waves crashing in on the north shore. I loved the sea; still do. For me it's the panacea to all ills and even now, in moments of crisis, I go to the sea and after a while I feel better. Grandad taught me the safety rules: never go down the steps to the beach when the tide is coming in. Never walk on, or lean over, the sea wall. I obeyed, as always. What I wanted was to hear the sounds of the sea and watch the waves come crashing in. I have always found the sea a solace, especially so during my solitary childhood. I had a playmate in my neighbour Sylvia, but otherwise spent a great deal of time alone.

'One day, Nana asked what I wanted to be when I grew up. I replied, 'Invisible.' Shocked, she mulled over this and then said, 'No one can be invisible, dear.'

'Then I'll be a seagull,' I replied.

Nana sighed. Little boys of the period wanted to be train drivers. Little girls wanted to get married or be nurses. What to do with a grandchild who wanted to be invisible or a seagull? Nearly twenty years later, my daughter, Paula, aged four, was asked the same question by her grandmother, Sybil Yates. The reply came without hesitation: 'Famous.'

It was to become an obsession that took control of her life and led her to disaster.

CHAPTER TWO

At a certain moment in my early childhood – I'm not sure of the year – I became very ill. I've never discovered what illness I had because at the time Gertrude was living on pills and sleeping twenty hours out of twenty-four, so she 'forgot' to send for the doctor. My father was a policeman and worked irregular hours. My life was saved by the unexpected arrival of Grandad George, who asked to see me. He told me much later that Gertrude couldn't reply when asked where I was, so he ran upstairs and found me half dead and delirious, crying that there were tigers on my bed. George scooped up all the bedclothes and me with them, put us in his car and drove hell for leather to his home. The family doctor was called and the entire household was mobilised to try to save me.

Some days later, I became aware of watery sunlight filtering through the window and lighting up a vase of snowdrops. I was warm in my high bed with its ladder that Grandad had made. Nana arrived with some beef tea. Terrified of being sick on the bed, I said I did not like beef tea. Nana replied, 'I made this, it's clean and it hasn't any fat in it.' I drank it all. I remember very little of the weeks that followed, except visits from the doctor and from my aunts, Connie and Marjorie. Everyone tried to make me eat, but in my child's mind eating was linked with images of slimy vegetables and fly-covered meat. I never ever wanted to eat. We had rationing until 1953, which further hindered my mother's disastrous attempts at cooking. To make things worse, Nana was an excellent cook, giving Gertrude another reason to resent her mother.

On the first day that I got out of bed, dressed and went downstairs, Nana decided on special means to revive my appetite.

'Bring the bottle George,' she said.

George brought in champagne, its label golden and impressive. Nana explained that champagne was for great occasions and royal coronations and this was a great occasion because we were celebrating my recovery. She handed me a small Venetian glass painted with pure gold spots and full of mysterious bubbles, and proposed the toast: 'To our Elaine.'

We all drank and I fell in love with the golden liquid that is one of the few things that my weak liver – still damaged by that childhood illness – allows me to drink. I was only allowed one glass, after which I was surprised to feel a bit hungry. Though money was tight, Nana was so charming that she was always able to get a bottle or two from a friend, even though it was very scarce. She rushed out of the room, returning with three bowls. In one, there was chicken soup, in the second, mashed potato and, in the third, thin strips of chicken breast.

'Eat whichever you want,' she said.

I ate all three of them and my recovery began, aided by occasional glasses of champagne, the adoring attention of my grandparents and visits from the elderly doctor, who was about to retire. He liked poetry and he taught me 'The Lake Isle of Inisfree' and 'Drake's Drum' and so entered into the legend that children invent about those who are important in their life. No one ever mentioned the fact that my hair had fallen out in large quantities during the illness, or that my fingers had become crooked and permanently deformed. Had I had rheumatic fever, or typhoid, as a New York iridologist once suggested? Or both?

Looking back, I realise that my grandparents were responsible for forming my rock-like stability which so helped me when under fire. They were a remarkable couple. He was 6 feet 5 inches in his socks, a retired police inspector and a former soldier in the Royal Artillery in the First World War. He came from the wild countryside of Bowland and his values were basic: truth, honour and the land. He once told me that the most important thing of all was the rich brown earth that he held in his hand. That was the essential in life.

Nana was 5 feet tall with pale green eyes and had a habit of tilting her head back and looking along her long nose at the object of her interest. She was from a brainy family who were comfortably off. Her father's hobby was buying terraced houses. One of her brothers was a chemist and another invented a patent medicine to combat flatulence. Her brother Herbert was a wise man with a penchant for the ladies. The family joke was that wherever Herbert went the population increased inexplicably. Then there was the black sheep of the family, who was a compulsive gambler and died very young. Nana loved opera and travel. She had a small collection of Venetian glasses that was wondrous and her perfume was Violette de Parme. I can still remember that fragrance now – it was just like having a cloud of violets floating over your head.

The passion of her life was George, who returned her feelings and never changed his mind, or his absolute devotion. He dreamed of teaching her to be economical, but it was not in her nature. She did try, once, when she bought 15 yards of damask for curtains and 15 yards to keep for the future, 'as an economy'. When he was told the price per yard, George staggered back as if shot and didn't say a word for hours. Nana thought she had best not try economising again.

The things I remember best about my grandparents were Nana's style, her iron will and her deep understanding of people's problems, especially mine, and of George I recall his rigour – 'military discipline, Elaine, military discipline'. I remember being taught to keep my word and best of all I remember watching them together. They were two beings in total harmony.

In the very long recuperation period after my illness, I stayed with my grandparents and was as happy as a princess. At home, I was forbidden to read in bed. 'You really must learn to sleep Elaine,' Gertrude woud say. During that period, she slept twenty pill-provoked hours a day and wanted a child who did the same. I was also forbidden to get up early or to go down to the kitchen to try to find something to eat. At Nana's house, George got up at a quarter to five each day as he had from childhood. He lit the fire, made two vast pots of tea and then began toasting bread. When I realised that I could get up, wash, dress and run down to the kitchen to sit in front of the fire with George, I was ecstatic. In winter, we stayed inside. In spring and summer, we walked in the garden, listening to the birds' dawn chorus and discussing life in general. My grandparents' views – his simple and honest; hers deeply perceived – have influenced my whole life and I believe they prepared me for its worst moments. Their stability became mine, so my early suffering became an advantage, the preparation for coping with a turbulent life.

In his book *The Ugly Ducklings,* the famous writer, psychiatrist and ethnologist, Boris Cyrulnik, cites a traumatic childhood as either the cause of lifelong neurosis or – for the artist – as a base for lifelong resilience. Whatever the foundation of my character, I have always been grateful to George and Constance for their wisdom and love, unfailingly given.

CHAPTER THREE

The other unforgettable character of childhood was Elizabeth, known as Polly, my great grandmother and Grandad's mum. He took me to see her as a special treat and once we stayed two nights in her little house. I had walked a long way with George and earned his praise and the title 'my little soldier'. I was happy and thrilled to think that we were going to stay with his mother. George was as proud of her as he was of me and said he wanted me to learn from her the valuable things in life: 'To love the earth, nature in its wild state, animals and the truth.'

Polly lived in a granite stone house in the Trough of Bowland area and was of farming stock. Under a thunder-grey sky, I returned to see the area again a year ago. Nothing had changed. The trees still leaned at an acute angle to the ground. The Roman walls still protected the fields and the hills were still mauve with heather. I sat near a stone bridge, eating a sandwich and thinking of Polly, who loved to laugh and had a killer instinct sense of humour greatly appreciated by her family.

She was eighty-eight when I first met her and still had gas lights in the house. Ever curious, I touched a white net bulb and to my horror saw it disintegrate. Terrified, I went to confess what I had done. Polly, quite unperturbed, said, 'You were just curious. You'd never seen one of those before had you? We'll go and put a new bulb in and then I'd best show you your room. You'll be wakened in the morning by a very good friend of mine.'

At five o'clock, as dawn lit the sky, a magnificent cock appeared on the stone wall of the garden and cockadoodled. It's funny how memories return at the most unexpected moments. I remembered him, years later, after the first of four eye operations in Cannes, when, at dawn, a cock in a nearby garden made such a noise a nurse cried, 'That cock should be shot!' Half stunned by medication, I said, 'Oh no, he reminds us all that this is a new day and we're going to get better.' The nurse liked this idea and told everyone. I hope he ends his life in old age and not as *coq au vin*!

The most memorable character from my childhood appeared when I was four or five. I was in the front garden picking marigolds when I saw a man at the gate. I had never seen anyone like him before and stared in wonder and admiration. This moment is as fresh now as ever it was, though six decades have passed since I met the gentleman. He was small, but had a rare elegance. His eyes were so heavy-lidded he seemed to be dozing and his hair was silvery white. I found this odd. He was not an old man like Father Christmas, who also had the white hair, because his face was relatively unlined. All this passed through my mind in a few seconds, while the stranger looked at me with as much curiosity as I looked at him. Then he spoke.

'You must be Elaine, may I come in?' I curtsied, because I was sure he must be royalty. Then I opened the gate.

After asking my mother's permission, the man took me to the local park and we went first to the hot houses, where he showed me rare orchids and carnivorous plants that thrilled me. Then he recited a poem to me. Then we went to the lake, where I was attacked by a gander. The gentleman tapped the gander with his silver-knobbed cane and I felt sure he was used to being obeyed, even by geese! He was cool, calm and tough beneath the elegant exterior. We went next to a café for tea and cakes and I told him that I was frightened that the Germans would drop bombs on our house. Mr X, as I shall call him, reiterated what Nana had already told me, that the Germans couldn't fly over Blackpool because of the tower, as their plane's wings would get tangled up in the metal parts. Reassured that he knew about things like that, I walked happily at his side back to the house. Outside the gate he said, 'I'll come again tomorrow.' And he did.

I was waiting for him in the garden, dressed in my best dress with a yellow ribbon in my hair. He handed me a bunch of violets that I kept for forty years, until long after they had disintegrated into powder. This time, we went to the town and walked along the promenade and then to see the Tower Aquarium, where I fell in love with the turtles. Once again, we had tea together and then we walked along the beach, so that I could give him a present, in return for the violets. I found a pretty shell, washed it carefully and handed it to him. I wonder if he kept it for as long as I kept the violets? As we neared the house, I took his hand in mine and looked up into his face. I was full of curiosity but didn't realise exactly what it was that I needed to know. I was simply touched, anxious to know him, or perhaps to impress.

During our absence, my other grandmother, Catherine, had arrived unexpectedly. The gentleman went into the kitchen with Gertrude and I went to say hello to my grandmother. Catherine was a very stern person with whom I was ill at ease. Nana wore silk georgette blouses and her perfume of violets, whereas Grandmother Catherine (my father Bill's mother) wore strictly tailored clothes and seemed to me to be grey both inside and out. She died not long afterwards, so perhaps she was already ill. I don't wish to do her an injustice, but her personality, to a small child, was in stark contrast to the charm and humour of her husband Robert, my paternal grandfather. Catherine was questioning me about where we had been, when I heard the sound of a kiss coming from the kitchen. In those days children didn't know about sex, but they always have had instincts that tell them things they aren't able to understand. I felt fear, because I knew that the visitor had kissed my mother in the kitchen and, worse, that Grandmother had heard it. I knew it was wrong without knowing why.

Minutes later, the man was seen out of the house by my mother and I went into the garden to watch him go. At the corner of the street he paused, turned and raised his hand to say goodbye and I ran like the wind to his side and looked anxiously into his face, wondering if he was going to say that he would come again and take me out. When he said nothing at all, I kissed his hand and he bent and kissed the top of my head. I never forgot him. When I was married, I searched for him, but records of the area of London where he had stayed were destroyed in the Blitz and he was not in the census of that period.

It was half a century before I discovered what I think, but cannot prove, is the truth about this man and what I learned, by a strange accident of destiny, only deepened the mystery and augmented my curiosity. Sometimes, when I remember his way of talking, his assured manner and those heavy, lidded eyes that seemed so calm, but perhaps were simply sensual, I have the impression of a man who saw beyond the façade of a person and understood what they felt, wanted, or needed. I am very grateful for my two meetings with the stranger. Better to have met, however briefly, the man you believe to be your real father than never to have met him at all.

CHAPTER FOUR

Bill was a kind, simple soul, who had played rugby in his youth and who collected clocks that he and I wound every Sunday to make sure they chimed on time. I don't remember a great number of happy times I had with Mum and Dad. Gertrude, or Trudie as she was sometimes known, was not a happy woman. Divorce simply wasn't an option in those days, so she and Dad were very much tied to one another. He suffered in silence from my mother's instability, her vituperations about his lack of desire for an argument and his habit of going to his allotment whenever she got too angry. On Sundays, Bill and I polished shoes, picked peas and green beans that Gertrude then boiled to a slime for lunch with the remains of the joint, including its trimming of flies' eggs. Until I was taught by my nana to remove maggots from everything, I was very often ill.

Bill and I had good times walking in Stanley Park, watching birds having a bath in a little rivulet, or the golfers walking round a nearby course. We laughed at their plus fours and the fact that they seemed to spend more time searching the bunkers, woodland and long grass for their ball than they ever did hitting it. These were moments of pleasure and calm in a difficult home life that worsened for me when I started school. A very quiet child, used to being alone, I hated school and for months I remained traumatised by it. I could see no reason to go there, because I already knew how to read, write and do simple arithmetic. Trudie was very proud of my intelligence, which she attributed to her heritage. My first reading at three was the Rupert books. Then I asked for something 'less childish' and was given *Peter Pan* and *Treasure Island*, both of which I read so many times I could recite them. *The Scarlet Pimpernel* by Baroness Orczy proved a bit difficult and Gertrude had to explain Sir Percy's masquerade to me. To please my mum, I also learned poems by the dozen: Browning, Tennyson, Flecker, Wilde and Shelley. I particularly loved 'The Lady of Shalott' and the lines of Coleridge about Kubla Khan, who lived in Xanadu 'Where Alph, the sacred river ran, Through caverns measureless to man'. As a child, I dreamed of faraway places and later I visited most of them. Books have always been a comfort when things haven't run smoothly.

My first teacher at school was a dear lady, Mrs Bell, who did her best to help me settle in. Then I moved on to a strange woman's class. She liked hitting children with the blackboard ruler. I lived in dread of her and the sewing lessons, when I unfailingly rendered her furious. My total incapacity to sew was only explained half a century later, when Monsieur, my French, second husband, informed me that I was left-handed, a 'changed over' left-hander. I didn't believe him, but my Aunt Marjorie confirmed that I had indeed been made to use my right hand before the age of two, because mum was trying to eradicate in me all resemblance to her mother. My daughter was also left-handed, as was a cousin, each left to their natural way of moving.

I often returned home from school with bleeding knees, having tried to hide from the rough boys in the playground and been thrown around for doing so. Gertrude didn't seem to notice and I washed my wounds, put TCP on them and said nothing. Then, one day, I arrived bleeding from both knees and one elbow. My grandparents were there and George asked what was wrong. When I explained, he fell silent. Then he said, 'Elaine, come with me.'

Nana cried out, 'George, I forbid you to teach that child unarmed combat. She's only five and she isn't strong enough yet.'

'Yes Mother,' he replied.

Then, he explained to me that in life certain people, who are cowards, like attacking those who are smaller or weaker than them. 'You have to defend yourself by using the element of surprise,' he continued, 'like Genghis Khan and his Mongols.'

At this point George let out a cry that frightened me and the neighbours' dog to death. The dog started barking and I was ashamed to want to run away, too.

'When you've given them a surprise, you hit them with the nearest heavy object,' George continued. 'There,' he indicated the nose.

The lesson continued for less than half an hour, but I learned enough to save my skin at least twice in my life, once when I was attacked by a group of Teddy boys and again in Antwerp, in my Bluebells days, as I was coming out of an alley. Then we returned to the house where Nana had taken over command of the kitchen so we could have afternoon tea.

A few days later, I was walking home from school, a distance of about a mile, when I found myself face to face with the two boys who had often injured me in the playground at school. I was terrified, but tried hard not to show it.

The elder of the two cried out, 'Let's break her legs.' I stayed where I was, eyeing the ground for a suitable, heavy object with which to defend myself. I could only see a smooth stone. I picked it up, delighted to have something to use as a weapon. The bigger of the two boys laughed out loud, 'What are you going to do with that?' Determined not to cry, I stood firm. Then, suddenly, he ran forward and kicked me on the shin. When he raised his fist to hit me, I hit first, an enormous, desperate blow on the nose. Then, seeing blood spurt out and hearing his screams of pain, I ran all the way home. I was relieved to find Grandad there with my mother and told them what had happened. George bandaged my leg and then sat pale and furious, looking out at the garden and plotting what to do.

I was eating a cake George had brought for me to have with my tea, when an irate lady knocked on the door. She was accompanied by her son, the horrible, aggressive boy. Grandad answered the door and stood stern faced listening to the woman's complaint. 'Your child, Elaine, attacked my son. I'm going to the police station. It's disgraceful, look, his nose is still bleeding.'

'Madam, your son has attacked my grandchild ever since she started school. Go home, or I shall ask my colleagues to come here and arrest him for assault.'

She said nothing at all, simply glowered at Grandad, as defiant as ever.

George continued, 'And if your son is tempted to hit Elaine again, please inform his father that ex-Inspector George Pye of the Blackpool Borough Constabulary will come personally to deal with him and he'll have reason to regret it.'

The lady and her bullying son hurried away and were not seen again in our street. Grandad looked down at me and said, 'Elaine, you defended yourself very well and I'm proud of you. Military discipline is important in life, especially when things are hard, and to have learned it by the age of five is remarkable. I shall tell Nana and she'll be proud of you, too. She'll probably decide it's a very important occasion and ask me to open a bottle of champagne. She does so love important occasions and I'm very happy that the champagne made you eat. We were worried that you'd never eat again.'

And I, who had always loved him, loved him even more.

At that time, Gertrude was unwell. She had begun to have attacks of rage that no one could explain. The reason was always the same: her hatred and jealousy of her mother, which had now achieved abnormal proportions, corroded her life and I became terrified that she would hate me, too, because Nana's eyes had reappeared in me. My way of talking and my excessive desire to give things to people who were poorer than I was were reminiscent of Constance and often my mother found life unbearable to have a child who was like the person she hated.

In hindsight, I think Gertrude's problems were more serious than the family realised. She was a wannabe who couldn't be. She wanted men to fall in love with her. She wanted to be famous. She wanted to be the most enchanting creature in the world. Like her mother. One of my great friends told me how he had fallen in love with Nana around 1960. I reckoned her age and said, 'But she was sixty odd at the time.' He looked at me as if I were mentally defective and said, 'Constance was perfect. She had no age. Just charm, charm and more charm.'

CHAPTER FIVE

To ease Gertrude's attacks of rage and panic, my grandparents thought it would be a good idea to take her on holiday. In wartime, the choice of destination was limited, but Nana had heard about a farm in the Isle of Man, where the food was marvellous and peace reigned. She and Grandad made all the arrangements. Mum would travel with us and Bill would come for his weekend off work and then return home. The family had never had any experience of mental illness and truly believed that a holiday would ensure that Gertrude would return home in the very best of health.

The night crossing was rough, but at dawn we all left the ship and made our way to the 'toast-rack' tram station so that we could travel to the farm and see a good stretch of the island at the same time. I can't remember what I thought of all this, except that I was excited by the idea of having my first holiday and I recall being fascinated by the fuschia hedges that bordered the tram track.

We arrived at last at the farm and were welcomed by the owner and his wife. Charles Kerruish looked like a Viking – blond, big and full of beans. He later became Speaker of the House of Keys, the lower house of the Tynwald, the Manx parliament. His wife was an excellent cook and we were all as happy as it was possible to be in wartime.

Of the holiday, I remember the exquisite beauty of Ballaglass Glen, where I wandered, often alone, filled with wonder. I remember Bill going into the shippon, a type of cattle byre, because he wanted to see Percy, Mr Kerruish's prize-winning bull. He had been warned not to go in there because Percy was going through a period of being bad tempered. What an understatement that proved to be. But, Bill's curiosity having got the better of him, he ambled over to inspect the monster, realising with something of a shock, that the door to Percy's stall was undone. Bill looked to the door and then to the unglazed shippon window that was used for tipping Percy's waste on to the manure mountain outside. He didn't have time for further reconnaissance, because Percy eyed him and not liking what he saw, charged.

I was outside, waiting for my dad to come back out when I saw him fly out of the shippon window and land in 6 feet of manure. Gertrude had hysterics and burst into machine-gun volleys of rebukes. Nana howled with laughter and so did I. Bill emerged finally from the manure heap and said ruefully, 'Well, Percy didn't like me! I'm lucky there was a window. Now I'd best go and take a bath, or I'll put everyone off their lunch.'

George smoked his pipe, calm as a judge and asked Gertrude to stop screeching. I took my shoes off because my feet were hot and promptly got a splinter embedded in my heel. No one could get it out, so Farmer Kerruish was called. He took one look at the splinter and went out, returning with a tall, blond-haired gentleman, who was one of the German prisoners of war interned on the island. The German was a doctor.

Everyone stared at the handsome man, who looked only at me. He spoke very quietly. 'I shall take out the splinter and I will try not to hurt. Are we ready?'

When he had removed the splinter, the doctor turned to Grandad and said, 'She is a very brave little girl.'

'I know,' Grandad replied, 'and I thank you, sir, for helping us.'

Nana was watching Mum, who stared after the doctor as if hypnotised. I was too young to understand what Nana had realised only too well.

The most vivid memory of the holiday was one whose effects were felt in my later life. The following morning, Gertrude took me to see the lighthouse at Maughold Head. It was a day when the sky was leaden, a storm lurking in the wings of life. The keeper of the lighthouse

showed us how it worked and let me wind the clock. Then
he said to Gertrude, 'Storm's brewing, madam, best return
to the mainland, or it'll be difficult for the little one to
cross over. The strip's narrow and a lot of folk won't visit
because of it.'

Gertrude hurried down the spiral staircase ahead of me
and left without a word of thanks. I watched as she ran
across the narrow strip of land, high above the sea that
smashed on the black rocks below. As Nana had taught me
to be a well-mannered little girl, I thanked the keeper and
began to walk slowly, carefully, towards the field on the
mainland while the keeper returned to the high tower. I
was halfway across, when a clap of thunder filled the air
and rain fell in torrents. Suddenly, I was terrified. Far
below, the sea made as much noise as the thunder and the
rain made it difficult to see and to move on the slippery
grass. I called for Gertrude to come and help me, but she
turned and ran hell for leather in the direction of the farm.
I never felt so alone and so frightened as at that moment.
I was seven years old, thin as a rake and shocked by the
disappearance of my mother. What to do?

Finally, I crawled on all fours towards the mainland,
sobbing uncontrollably, until suddenly, I felt myself lifted
on to Grandad's shoulders and heard Bill say, 'Thank God
we came George.' Grim-faced, they helped me to the field.
There, Bill threw a blanket over me and George carried me
back to the farm, where Nana put me in the bath and then
to bed. I cried all afternoon until Bill came and told me

one of my favourite stories from the very early days of my childhood, about Quacker, the little yellow duck, who lived in Stanley Park. I was unaware at that time that Grandad had gone after my mother, who had locked herself in her room. Nana told me he had threatened her with a court order if she continued to neglect me.

When we returned to the mainland, Gertrude's condition worsened and a family conference was held with my grandparents' doctor, who said it was urgent that Trudie be sent to see a psychiatrist. Further family meetings were held when she absolutely refused to agree. Finally, it was decided that she must be kept in her room during the daytime with the door locked. I checked the lock before going to school and a member of the family fed and kept an eye on her during the day. At night, Grandad and Bill did the honours.

At weekends I tried hard to interest my mum in her favourite radio programme 'Much Binding in the Marsh' with Kenneth Horne and Richard Murdoch. I could do nothing to neutralise her hate-orientated nature, or the pathological jealousy of her mother that was ruining her life. An unforgettable moment in my young days occurred one spring afternoon when Gertrude was recounting her 'abominable childhood' to some friends: 'I was made to scrub floors night and day. I was bought clothes from the second-hand counter in the market. I slept on the floor and cried for my mother when she and George went out dancing.'

The friends looked outraged, until a defiant voice rang

out, 'You are a liar Trudie, a most disgusting, wicked liar! You were spoiled to death because you were my mum's first child and you had the most wonderful clothes. My sister and I only ever had your cast-offs. I remember one of your dresses, the one you wore for your first ball. It was the most beautiful dress I ever saw and I envied you. Now take back what you said, what you always say to get pity and make folk hate my mum. If you don't take it back, I shall tell my father and George will know how to deal with you.'

The friends left quietly, leaving Gertrude and her youngest sister, Connie, face to face. Connie was the most beautiful of the sisters with her big China-blue eyes and her curly, blonde hair. She was afraid of no one and stood her ground with my mother. Gertrude sat down on a stool, silent, her eyes empty of all expression. She had retreated to the no-man's land that was her catatonic refuge from reality, that inner landscape only she could see. 'Come with me,' Connie said, and to my joy I was taken to my grandparents' house 'for a few days'.

Gertrude's strange behaviour came to a head one day when she was trying to clean the house. That day, her sister Marjorie was keeping an eye on her as it was the weekend. While Marjorie cleared the kitchen and washed the breakfast things, Gertrude looked at me and said, 'Put the plug into the socket,' and she handed me the vacuum lead. As I was putting the plug in the socket, she threw a bucket of water on the floor under my feet. I shot up in the air and landed near the kitchen, dazed, terrified and unaware that my life had been saved by a pair of comic, wooden-soled shoes given to me for my birthday by my Aunt Connie. I was also unaware that Grandad was standing in the doorway and had seen everything. In shock, I vaguely remember a terrible exchange between him and my mother. Then I was carried out to the car where Nana wrapped me in the car rug. When I had been examined by the doctor, I was put to bed. Another family conference was held and it was a long time before I heard the doctor's car driving off. I wondered what had happened and closed my eyes, trying to make the fear go away, but it stayed. Then the door opened and Nana arrived and sat in the armchair reading. I slept at once.

This incident heralded the worse part of my mother's illness, which lasted for fifteen months. Liza Minnelli once recounted how she became her mother's guardian during Judy Garland's health problems. I remember feeling that Gertrude and I had changed places and I was the mother and she the child. Whenever I saw her, I tried to be reassuring. I wrote poems to please her, but she fell easily into a violent state of panic. I shall never know what caused Gertrude's symptoms, but I've often wondered if a far distant ancestor who was 'a genius but mad as a hatter', according to family legend, had left an unwelcome genetic gift? Was it possible that Gertrude suffered from schizophrenia?

CHAPTER SIX

By the time my mother had recovered from her breakdown, I was in many ways grown up. The few fond memories I have – going shopping, or wandering around the flower market – are tinged with an edginess, which always stopped me from fully relaxing in her company. I had skipped adolescence and its problems and leaped from child to woman. I was eleven years old, settled and very happy in my new school.

Elmslie was an exclusive establishment that had been founded by Elizabeth Brodie and was run by her and her sister, Miss Peggy, who did the cooking for pupils at lunchtime. The fees were high and they gave only seven free scholarships each year. As we were not rich, I dreamed of being one of those free pupils. I had gone for an interview and entrance examination when I was ten, a priceless occasion for me.

Elizabeth Brodie was a great lady of venerable appearance, her white hair lightly waved on either side of her head. Behind the deceptively gentle exterior, she had a razor-sharp brain of great originality. She began by asking why I wanted to come to the school and I replied truthfully, 'I want to come here because Elmslie is different.'

'Why is it different?'

'It teaches all the usual subjects that ordinary schools teach, but here you encourage the girls to visit the opera, the ballet, the theatre and the cinema. I want to know all that so I shan't be as ignorant as I am now.'

Miss Brodie stared at me as if I'd sprouted big ears like Mr Spock. Then she handed me a paper with questions. I filled it in as quickly as I could, afraid to lose her interest. Miss Brodie glanced at the paper, then at me and said, 'You are accepted Elaine.'

'What about the entrance examination?'

'You passed it already,' she replied. 'Now I shall introduce you to my sister who organises our delicious lunches.'

'I don't like eating,' I replied.

Miss Peggy appeared, an enigmatic smile on her face. 'If you don't like what I make, you can leave it all,' she said.

I loved her, Miss Brodie, the school, everything, from that moment on. Elmslie was based in an old manor house, with tooled leather walls on the ground floor and an impressive mahogany staircase leading up to the first floor. The grounds were lined with elms, hence the name, and were reserved for games and sports days. I still remember my first lunch in the main hall with the other children who lived too far away to return home at midday. Miss Peggy announced cottage pie to be followed by apple crumble. Wary of food, I tasted a tiny forkful of the cottage pie before eating it all plus a second plateful. I plead the Fifth Amendment as to how many plates of crumble I demolished and this *tour de force* of eating led to interesting results. When I first went to the school, I was 4 feet 10 inches tall. Two years later, I had grown amazingly and was 5 feet 5 inches and still growing like Jack's famous beanstalk. Miss Peggy congratulated me more than once on my appetite and years later I remember her, her sister, Miss Bothwell, our French teacher, Miss Cantlay, our maths professor and Miss Beamer, our English teacher, with the greatest affection and respect.

On my way home from school each day, I used to call at my Aunt Marjorie's house to see her baby. For years I'd longed for a sister and when Diane was six weeks old, I told her that I could be her sister-cousin, if she liked the idea. In the beginning, I had gone home and shared the joy of Diane's presence with my mum, but Trudie had started to hate the baby, her corrosive jealousy of anyone I loved making her ill with loathing. She hated Diane to the end of her days, though there has never been a kinder or more gentle person than my cousin. Looking back, I think Gertrude wanted to be exactly like her own mother, who was loved by everyone. As she couldn't be Nana, she hated anyone and everyone who provoked love. To protect my sister-cousin from Mum's anger, I had taken to visiting the house either after school, or on a Saturday morning with Bill. I was unaware that Gertrude often hid behind a car at the bottom of the street, timing how long I spent with the baby.

On Diane's second birthday, I arrived with flowers for my aunt and a tiny bar of chocolate for my cousin. I was delighted to find my Uncle Reginald there, his face wreathed in smiles because one of his friends, with whom he had 'done the war' in France, Italy and North Africa, had sent him a Camembert. He was about to investigate the Camembert when Gertrude arrived. Marjorie handed her sister a cup of tea. Reginald unwrapped the cheese and the room was filled with the stink of dirty socks. Marjorie fled to the kitchen without a word.

My mother said, 'You really are a disgusting degenerate Reg. How can you swallow such filth?'

Reginald smiled as Gertrude followed her sister to the kitchen. I stared at the Camembert and Reginald cut a slice of bread and handed me a small wedge of the cheese. 'At least you have enough instinct to taste things before you start complaining!'

It was delicious and we finished a large wedge of the cheese between us. Then I went upstairs to see Diane. Hearing the back door of the house slam, I looked out of the window and saw my mum rushing away in fury. Exhausted by her anger and her moods, I sat on the little chair near the cot and told my sister-cousin how much I loved her. Diane slept on, as little children do and after a while I went downstairs, hugged my aunt and uncle and walked slowly home.

I was just inside the door when Gertrude pounced on me and pushed me into a narrow broom cupboard. I heard the lock turn and wondered how long it would be before my father came home from duty. Gertrude was still enraged that I had eaten the cheese with my uncle and shouted, 'I hope you die! You're a degenerate like all the rest of the family. I'm ashamed of you.'

It was morning before she let me out, soaked in sweat and urine. She stared at me as if waiting for some response, but I remained silent. I went upstairs, took clean clothes from my room and went to the bathroom to wash. I was unaware that this incident had changed my attitude towards Gertrude. Before, because I loved my mum and wanted her to love me, I had tried to please, to pacify, to be what she wanted me to be. I'd sat for hours under the burning hot dryer having my hair permed in Aunt Connie's hair salon, so my mother could dream of my resemblance to Shirley Temple. Shirley Temple I am not and I never was! I'd kept quiet when she invented reasons to row with my dad. I'd gone out alone from the age of four to stand looking at the sea that was my only respite from the emotional storms at home. Now, in the space of twenty-four hours, I changed and from that day on I treated Gertrude with affection, but remained distant in my heart. I humoured her and did what she wanted within reason, but she could no longer touch the armour of my determination to survive.

When I was clean, I went downstairs and Gertrude, longing for a row, as always, shouted, 'I'm ashamed of you!'

I replied very softly, 'And I am ashamed of you.'

She collapsed in a chair, her eyes staring into space. She had again retreated into the catatonic state that she assumed when she had done wrong. Her body was immobile, her black eyes empty. This retreat into an untouchable place was to become more and more familiar and I accepted that there was nothing to be done, so I walked to the promenade and watched the sea coming in. The sea was my sedative, the reality of power and beauty and I returned home renewed, despite everything.

My religious upbringing in childhood was to say the least odd. I often went to the synagogue with Nana and her two Jewish women friends with whom she had 'shown solidarity and bugger Hitler!' during the war. On Sundays, I went to the Methodist, Baptist or Church of England Sunday School, depending which one was in favour with Gertrude at the time.

I remember going on a Church of England trip to a nearby abbey with a little friend who lived next door. Gertrude had given me two pennies to spend. My friend, Marie, had no money, so I gave her one of my pennies and we both had fun buying postcards to give to our parents when we got home. The pleasure of giving has always been one of my needs. Unfortunately, on this occasion, it made Gertrude furious. Realising that the postcards I had given her could only have cost one penny, she asked where the second penny was and howled like a banshee when I said I'd given it to Marie. When Bill rose to defend me, Gertrude ran to the bathroom 'to cut my wrists'. She had threatened suicide for years and from the age of four I had had the habit of kneeling down on the floor outside the bathroom to see if any blood was pouring out.

Bill and I sat in silence, both of us aware that Gertrude would be unable to switch off her anger and I would suffer her recriminations about the penny for weeks, if not months, to come. The episode confirmed for me the pleasure of sharing and also the necessity for limiting anger to five minutes and not going on and on for ever when displeased. All negative things have their positive side and Gertrude's desire to continue her attacks of rage taught me that I can show anger if I want to, but after a five-minute bellow, I shut up.

CHAPTER SEVEN

In the early fifties – I can't remember exactly when – Gertrude first saw a television set and its flickering black-and-white images. It was in the window of a shop in Blackpool's town centre. Entranced, she stood there, as if hypnotised, in the freezing cold of an early spring day. On the promenade, the sea was crashing against the massive cement walls. A few hardy day trippers were walking, mauve-nosed, along Church Street in the direction of the pier. Gertrude was oblivious to her surroundings. Finally, I said, 'Shall we go home Mum, I'm cold.'

'I want one of those,' she replied and hurried into the shop. She came out minutes later, her face pale with shock, having learned the price of the desired object. 'I want one, but they cost a fortune.'

Gertrude was silent on the way home and, feeling sorry for her, I linked arms and tried to take her mind off her frustration. Bill was already laying the table for tea. Gertrude looked at him and said, 'I've seen television.'

'It's very interesting isn't it,' Bill replied. 'I hadn't seen it until the other day when Jack Long let me watch his for five minutes. It was a very interesting programme and I'd have liked to see it to the end.'

'They cost a fortune.'

'I know they do, but perhaps someday they'll get cheaper.'

Day after day, Gertrude went to watch television in the town-centre shop. Sometimes, she stood soaked to the skin in a downpour, ignoring everything except the images on the screen. Finally, determined to take her mind off this new mania, I suggested a ride on the promenade tram to Fleetwood. Gertrude liked trams and going to the street market or the fishermen's stalls on the quay. For a moment, she seemed to have forgotten the television. Then, on arrival, as we stepped down and I began to walk towards the port, I found myself alone. Looking back, I saw Gertrude staring fixedly at a poster near the tram stop. I hurried back and looked at the poster that had captured her attention. It said: Talent Contest – First Prize: a television set. Entry forms can be collected at the Tourist Office.'

Gertrude rushed off to find out what we must do to enter. I ran after her, but she was supersonic. By the time I arrived at the Tourist Office, she was already out and brandishing an entry form. She filled it in as if her life depended on it.

'You'll win the television set,' she said.

There was genuine excitement about the arrival of television at the time and everyone wanted one. My heart sank down into my shoes and terror filled me. If I didn't win, I knew I would never hear the end of it. I had no experience of talent contests and didn't know what this entailed. I watched, resignedly, as Gertrude went back to the office and handed in the form. Her face was flushed and she was on some strange inner overdrive. I wished, as so often at those times of my mum's curious behaviour, that I could be at Nana's house, picking roses in the garden, eating home-made cakes, or learning about butterflies and other natural things from George. If I were there, George and I would walk down to the sea and I would pick sea-pinks by the dozen and put them in vases and old jam jars.

I had no beautiful clothes, just an outfit that Gertrude and I had chosen in a local shop. She wanted me to wear bright red, her appalling bad taste – a joke in the family – coming to the fore when she imagined me on stage. I chose another colour, paler, more mysterious, and off we went to the contest. It was not a bathing-suit competition. Instead, each contestant had to step up on stage where she was framed from the waist up in a giant replica of a television set. She became the picture and she had to talk for a few minutes to the audience. Most of the contestants were not used to being on stage, so I had the advantage of having learned my craft in theatre shows when I was small. I have no recollection what I said, but I know the audience laughed a lot. Probably, I recounted the story of my mum being hypnotised by the television set in the shop in Bank Hey Street.

All the contestants had to walk on stage for the result to be announced. Grandad had driven us there and most of the family were present. When I won, Gertrude burst into tears of pride and joy and cried out, 'That's my daughter!'

In the car on the way home, I felt tired, happy to have won, but in serious need of a quiet corner. My mouth was dry and I was exhausted by the relief from the tension.

'Would you mind if Elaine came for the weekend?' Grandad asked, 'then, when I bring her back, I'll deliver your television for you. I suppose the *Gazette* will want to send a photographer to take pictures of Elaine next week.'

Gertrude said yes with enthusiasm and half an hour later I was sitting in front of the fire at my grandparents' house, drinking tea and eating a slice of pie. Grandad smiled his slow, knowing smile and Nana said, 'You were very good, Elaine, and I'm glad you won, but George felt it would be best if you came here, because Gertrude will talk even in her sleep about the television set!'

I put on my winceyette pyjamas and climbed up the ladder to my bed. There were books by the lamp and my favourite yellow roses in a bowl. I was too tired to read and slept at once. The house on the estuary was peaceful, just the ticking of Nana's grandmother clock and the cry of a night bird in the darkness.

What followed the publication of my photo in one of the papers was a period of change. Entranced by the television set, Gertrude was temporarily silent. Then we began to get pornographic letters with drawings of giant willies that took even Gertrude's mind off the television. Then two men began to pursue me. One was an elegant type, who just happened to be on the tram each day when I travelled home from school.

'Come with me,' he said, 'I'll be with my chauffeur one day and we'll take you for a ride.'

I didn't really understand what his intentions were, but one day, when he grabbed my wrist, I hurried away from the tram, leaving my tennis racquet behind. Gertrude immediately accused me of losing it deliberately, which was very unjust, as I adored playing tennis with my Uncle Reginald in Stanley Park. She never bought me another racquet and continued with her recriminations for months. Bill and I disappeared to the allotment when she started screaming. I found her exasperating, and I couldn't bear to see my father upset by her.

The second man was more dangerous, because he was the husband of a friend of my mother's. He picked me up from school one day and said, 'Hop in, Elaine. It's pouring down and you'll be soaked. I'll take you home.'

He didn't. Instead, he drove me to Fleetwood and

threatened to drive off the jetty and into the sea if I didn't do what he asked. I leaped out of the car and into the water and ran all the way home. Gertrude asked me what had happened and why I arrived home soaked to the skin. I told the truth, but she didn't believe me. Suddenly enraged, she ran into the garden, collided with a large frog, panicked and fell against the rockery cutting her face.

Bill tended her face and comforted her howling. Unable to stand any more, I left home and walked all the way to Nana's house, arriving at nightfall. My grandparents asked no questions, just put me in the bath, fed me and helped me to settle in my bed. Then Grandad drove to Blackpool to see Mum. He believed my story. She never did.

As I didn't want to go straight back home, I stayed with my grandparents for some time and every morning George drove me to school and was there waiting for me at the end of the afternoon. He was sitting in the car, when a child ran out from behind a bus into the road and was killed by an oncoming vehicle. I was there, too, and saw the contents of her head seep on to the road. I let George lead me back to his car and then, without a word, go back to check that the child's body was covered and that the police and ambulance services had been called.

That was my first experience of sudden death and I was in shock. I was instantly fearful of death and made horribly aware of my vulnerability. I kept telling myself that I was Grandad's little soldier and must therefore be brave, but my whole body shook and I felt curiously light headed.

George drove home and, after a word with Nana, took me into the kitchen and stood in front of the fire.

'You saw someone die today, Elaine, and you're shocked. That's why you're trembling. It's normal when human beings are shocked. I suggest you eat something, even if you don't feel hungry. Then we'll walk down to the sea. That always makes us feel better, doesn't it?'

Nana served a lovely meal with vegetables from the garden, a big white fish and a mound of purée potatoes. I kept closing my eyes in the hope that the seeping brains would disappear but I realised that they would remain until time dulled the memory.

CHAPTER EIGHT

When the time came to choose a career, I wanted to be a doctor. Gertrude had hysterics for a week and seemed to be heading for another nervous breakdown. In the end, she simply refused to allow it and enrolled me, after O Levels, in a three-year course at the local technical college and school of art. I couldn't understand her bizarre reaction. Neither could anyone in the family, except Nana, who kept silent, though she seethed with anger. The course I had to take was intended to prepare me for the career Gertrude desired me to follow. She wanted above all that I should become a civil servant. Uncle Reginald called her a damned fool and remarked that anyone less likely to become a civil servant than me would be difficult to find. Gertrude ignored everyone. She also thought it likely that

I would marry young – a titled man, or a prince, of course! It was during this period that I learned to cut myself off from being affected by mad, bad or destructive personalities. It was an invaluable lesson that I've often needed in my life.

For the first three months, I was the dud of the class in shorthand and even worse at typing. Then, I heard that the college did evening classes as well as the full time courses. If I could cram for a year, morning, noon and night, I wondered if I could pass the three-year course in one year. I had already decided to leave after a year and asked Mr Taylor, my teacher, to help me speed up. I thank him all these years later for having had the patience of Job with my mangling of typewriters and hieroglyphic-like shorthand. Finally, I passed all the exams Gertrude had thought necessary for a budding civil servant, but having seen an ad in *The Stage* magazine for Bluebell Girls, I announced to my mother that I was going to audition for Miss Bluebell in Manchester and that she must accompany me as I was under age. If I couldn't be a doctor, I had decided to make the best of things and see the world and earn some money at the same time. Ten years of ballet, tap, modern ballet and mime classes had prepared me for just that.

For the audition I wore a violet leotard and black tights. Miss Bluebell was a tough Liverpudlian with a veneer of Parisian elegance. Her hair was expertly tortoiseshelled and her perfume was Mitsouko. She was supremely hard working, highly motivated, astute and ruthless. She seemed pleased by my appearance, asked only to see the simplest of steps and then told me I was too young to go to Paris without a chaperone and that I would have to wait a few months before joining the European leg of the Lido's World Tour, after its return from South America. I later learned that the spectacular show based on the Lido presentation, but redesigned for theatres all over the world, had been so expensive to mount that the owners never sent out a tour again. They kept the troupe in Las Vegas for a while, but it was nothing like on the scale of the luxurious show in which I took part. It was a unique experience and I'm so glad I did it.

Gertrude was overawed by Miss Bluebell, who marched over to her and said, 'Elaine dances well, she's the right height and she's beautiful, but she's too young. She can't join the troupe until next September. I shall send for her.'

Before Gertrude could reply, Miss Bluebell had disappeared in a cloud of perfume, with a brief smile in my direction. That year, Gertrude entered me for beauty contests everywhere. Her desire to compete via me stood me in good stead many years later when I was a novelist in the US. In New York, everyone competes and no one needs a psychiatrist if they lose, even though the city is full of them. People just try again and do better in order to win the next time. It's a good attitude to have. In France, where I now live, folk hate competition and try everything to avoid it. In England, I don't remember any great hostility in the beauty business, apart from the occasion when one girl who cut up my swimsuit before a major contest. A sponsor appeared, gave me a whole range of swimwear and I won. Thank you Windsor Woolies.

It was at the televised national final of an inter-resort competition that I first met Jess Yates. He took photos of me and followed me around with avid curiosity. It never occurred to me that I was beautiful. Boys had pestered me before, but I always preferred older men. When it was all over and I had won, I went to the dressing room to change. I was about to slide out of the swimsuit, when Jess walked in and asked if he could continue taking pictures. I said no. He stayed. I wouldn't take off the swimsuit while he was there and finally told him to leave. He stayed. So I pushed him outside, changed quickly and hurried back to my mother and the head of publicity for the town of Blackpool, who were my chaperones.

'I detest that man,' I said to my mother.

'You must be nice to him, he's from the BBC,' she replied dispassionately.

I didn't see him again for two years and I didn't want to. I was just proud and happy to have won a major contest for my home-town resort. I loved my home town and I still do.

At the end of the season, I went with Gertrude to see some of the touring shows being previewed at the Opera House before opening in London. In previews over the years, we had seen Mae West in *Diamond Lil,* the unforgettable Evelyn Laye in *September Tide* and Leonide

Massine, at the end of his career, dancing the leading role in *Petrouchka*. Trudie loved the theatre and pretended to be Evelyn Laye for weeks. I, too, adored the theatre, but I never wanted to be anyone but me, nor ever thought I could be. I still wanted to be invisible but had realised that it might be difficult. I provoked curiosity and often aggression with my habit of ignoring impertinent questions. In those days, I still thought I had the right to live my life without interrogation from complete strangers.

Finally, I won the contest that had obsessed Gertrude for years, the *Gazette & Herald* Miss Blackpool. She had entered me the previous year, lying as usual about my age. To my horror, I was disqualified. When I re-entered, I won. Mum was unaware that it was the last time I would enter a contest at her instigation. I was due to leave for Paris and viewed the future with uncertainty. Would I survive the unknown? I thought the idea of having a holiday away from Gertrude was fine, but was very upset at the idea of leaving Bill and my grandparents. Still, I had an intense curiosity about people and places. I was a blank canvas waiting to be painted by those around me. I didn't yet realise that my childhood and some of its horrors had made me difficult for ordinary people to understand. My habit of living my life on many levels – superficially, deep thoughtful, defensive, creative and invisible, yet seeming outwardly calm – would make it difficult for people to pigeonhole such an enigmatic character. I shouldn't have been so concerned with people's reactions. I should have been more concerned by the realisation that I am the living phantom of the child in the cemetery at the beginning of this book and be proud that I survived childhood with my brain and my sense of humour intact. Gertrude waved a tearful goodbye at the station and I promised to write every day, which I did. Despite our difficult relationship, she was my mum and I loved her. Years later, with Paula, I would learn once again that the mother-daughter bond is very strong. I was upset by Trudie's tears and nearly cancelled the whole thing, but I needed to grow up and instinct told me that I must live my life and let my mum live hers.

On arrival in Paris, in late 1956, I took a taxi to the hotel in the rue La Boetie where I had been told to report. I had realised with horror that I couldn't understand a word of French and felt isolated by the lack of communication. Traffic whizzed noisily by on the wrong side of the road. It was raining, the air was grey, the buildings grey and my nervous system felt pretty grey, too. The hotel was off the Champs-Elysées, near the Lido, where we would rehearse. We also used the former bar, the Bal Tabarin in Pigalle and the Empire Theatre in the Avenue Wagram.

There were nine complicated routines to learn in twenty-one days, plus endless changes of wigs, shoes and costumes to go with them, as well as a whole new philosophy of living and working and being to understand. Rehearsals were from nine in the morning until seven in the evening with barely a break. I realised immediately that my testing time had come.

After rehearsals, I ate with some of the other girls in a little restaurant, the Etoile Verte, in the rue Brey; two giant plates of goulash and then two helpings of bananas and cream. This was the only real meal of the day, apart from a French breakfast and hard-boiled eggs bought for lunch from a bar in the Lido Arcade. I had never been a big eater and wrote reams to my mother telling her about my new and prodigious appetite. At this time, I lived in terror of forgetting the routines, or worse, of falling on my backside when walking down the vast staircases that were a spectacular feature of the stage sets for the show. I never went on dates and felt afraid in the streets because everyone wanted to talk to me and I was completely unused to contact with total strangers who chattered so fast it was like machine-gun fire. It took three weeks for me to venture a word and then I never stopped!

In between rehearsals we had to go for costume and shoe fittings. The showgirls all had lovers and gossiped interminably about them while being fitted with their costumes. They appeared half nude and did not dance; they showed. All of them were exquisite and spoilt by the richest men in Europe, the most popular girl being the one with huge square nipples. The girls talked of nothing but shopping and meeting their boyfriends. Sometimes, they decided to change them for new models. Once in a while, they discussed the sexual foibles of their men friends, which left me open mouthed in wonder. Men who wanted to be beaten up, covered in cream and eaten, imagine!

The Bluebells of those days danced fully clothed, often in 3-foot high wigs and the beautiful costumes of Folco and Fost, the renowned Lido designers. Like the showgirls, they were pursued for their class, their seeming inaccessibility and their beauty. Their preoccupations in life were quite different from those of the showgirls. Each Bluebell worried about whether the tall, heavy wigs and head-dresses would cause her hair to fall out, which it often did. She suffered pain from the iron crinoline cages that left giant bruises on thighs and hips and she courted broken ankles dancing and descending steep staircases in 4-inch heels. But it was all accepted as good experience. Most girls developed a superhuman resilience to pain, fatigue, difficult conditions and being followed night and day by panting men in the street. There were three of us new girls. The established Bluebells looked on newcomers as something to be tolerated, nothing more. I was so nervous about the routines, but they were helpful during rehearsals, although they kept us greenhorns at a distance on a personal level.

I was next to the youngest in the troupe and did my best to watch and learn. I barely spoke to anyone until the day, just before our last week of rehearsal, when we were trying out the dances with our costumes on. I was told by one of the girls to dress in the corridor because of the lack of room. Annoyed, I snatched the towel from the make-up table and everything fell on the floor; bottles broke, clouds of powder filled the air. At that moment, I heard the door creak and, turning, I came face to face with a black-haired man who had opened the door with his cane. His eyes were as dark as his hair and they held mine, his curious, mine furious. Then he moved away down the corridor. It was my first view of the unforgettable character who inspired one of my most successful novels, *Some Women Dance*.

Fraternisation with the personnel of the Lido was forbidden, but it happened from time to time. I listened to gossip and thoroughly enjoyed it, but didn't think about taking a lover. The thought of going home pregnant was far too terrifying. At one point, I was followed with great enthusiasm by a millionaire with a lopsided head and a Facel Vega, a beautifully made sports car. Wherever I went, Gaston appeared, invited me to lunch and I said no. Then, just before our departure from Paris, I accepted a lunch date, hoping he would take me to one of the fancy restaurants in the Champs-Elysées. Instead, he drove me out of Paris to Ville d'Avray, which has a lake that was painted by Corot. There are some beautiful houses facing the lake and one of them was our destination.

We ate in a private room and I told Gaston all about rehearsals, costume fittings and the showgirls who had lovers by the dozen. He turned scarlet from excitement and I wondered if he had had too much wine and whether he would be able to drive us back to Paris. I drank only water and felt increasingly ill at ease in what I thought was a very odd kind of restaurant. The room had erotic etchings on the walls and a bed draped in plum velvet in the corner. I was unaware that I was actually in a de-luxe brothel which, in addition to lots of beautiful girls, served four-star food in private rooms for those rich enough to pay for it.

At the end of the meal, Gaston threw off his jacket, got out his penis and lunged at me. I leaped up from the banquette and asked him what he thought he was doing.

'I love you,' he said, 'and I am going to ravish you.'

I had had no experience of outlandish declarations of love from men and certainly never from one with whom I had just had my first long conversation. Neither had I ever linked love and rape. Terrified, I rushed out of the room where I collided with a blonde in frilly knickers and a negligée. 'Calm down,' she said, 'I'm your friend. Come downstairs with me.'

'I want to go back to Paris immediately,' I replied.

Suddenly I was surrounded by cooing girls, who gave me coffee and chocolates and admonished a sheepish-looking Gaston for bringing such an inexperienced nitwit to an establishment like that. Giggling like schoolgirls, they reassured me and continued pretending to chide Gaston, who by this time was thoroughly enjoying himself. I had never heard of a brothel and still didn't realise that these darling girls were there to look after the other super-rich, lopsided heads of the region. Gaston was very gentlemanly. He drove me back to Paris, bowed and left me outside my hotel. I never saw him again.

I was about to enter the hotel, when I saw the dark man

with the walking stick watching me from the rear of a sleek, black car. He didn't speak. He didn't smile. He just looked at me with a kind of hypnotising force. Out of my depth but interested, I ran into the hotel and disappeared into my room. Then, from my window on the fourth floor, I watched the black car disappearing into the distance. I wondered who he was and what he was, without really wanting to know. He was my mystery man and I preferred the intangible to the familiar.

Before leaving Paris, we all had our photos taken at the famous Harcourt Studios. I hated mine. It shows a simpering twit, which is what I surely was. We were also taught that Bluebell Girls were always elegant, always beautifully dressed with 6-inch heels. I wandered around near the Bal Tabarin one day and found a wonderful shop, Ernest, selling the highest of high heels. Entering, I was immediately spoilt to death, assisted, given a coffee and generally indulged by the owner and four other female clients, who were even taller than me. They left before I did and I chose two pairs of suitable stilts.

'It's not often that I meet girls that tall,' I said to the cashier.

'Oh they're boys from the cabaret at Madame Arthur,' she replied.

Walking back to the hotel I felt suddenly homesick. In Paris girls were boys and boys were girls and for many night was day. I'd encountered pantomime dames before, but this was all very thrilling and avant garde. I felt so alone and none too confident to face the future.

We were to travel by train to Antwerp for the opening of the tour. I was passing through the barrier, when I saw the man with the walking stick at the other side. When I paused before him, he spoke to me for the first time.

'You'll be changed when you come back from this experience. At the moment you are beautiful, but too young for me. Someday we'll meet again. In a few years' time, you'll be perfect for my tastes. I shall keep in touch. I shall never lose sight of you.' With that he walked away, out of my life, or so I thought. His name was Gianni, a powerful presence, but to my eyes a mystery that I would never be able to unravel. Half of me wanted to run after him. The other half wanted to run in the opposite direction. As he'd said, I was too young, for the moment.

On arrival in Antwerp, the high heels proved to be tricky, as it had snowed early that year, then frozen over and the temperature was well below zero. The girls immediately organised lifts from local people to avoid the possibility of doing triple salkos in their 6-inch heels on the edge of the quayside. Men of all shapes, sizes and ages came to ferry us to the theatre half a mile away. All of them were gentlemen, given the pure reputation of the troupe. The purity publicity angle was a touch of genius either by the publicist of the Lido, or Miss Bluebell herself. An astute businesswoman, who sought class above all in her girls, she knew the value of inaccessibility, even if it were not always true. The reality was that the girls were all beautiful, sensual and even if innocent, like me, were extremely interested in leaving their innocence far behind.

We stayed in the best hotel in town, but found it hard to sleep because of strange noises coming from the floorboards. We soon discovered that although it had an elegant reputation, the hotel was infested with rats. Despite the problems of snow, the freeze-up and rats, rehearsals resumed and then, at last, the evening of the première arrived. Miss Bluebell, whose legendary energy and inspiration had made her name and her élite team of girls famous, gave the assembled company a tough pep talk.

I wrote a letter to my mother telling her I was shaking with fear. Though we were hundreds of miles apart and I was becoming ever more independent, the mother-daughter bond still made me want to share my news with Trudie. I soon forgot my fear when the curtains lifted, the orchestra struck up the overture and the entire company, elegant in white with crystal embroidery, moved forwards to open the show. At this moment, I remembered the day when Miss Bluebell had kept me behind after rehearsals to teach me how to walk down the steep stairs like a princess without staring in myopic fascination at my feet. She had said 'Do it again dear' for what seemed like hours and I, half dead from tiredness, had descended and then remounted the stairs, feeling like murdering her at every exhausted step. But I learned once and for always, and this opening night I was very grateful for the time she'd spent on me. I also learned that absence due to ill health was sufficient reason for the annulment of a contract. I worked, therefore, with a broken elbow in Vienna and pneumonia in Munich. Those who began the eight-month tour as untried girls ended it as women of the world, capable of running the gamut of any catastrophe without flinching, or running home to Mummy. I shall always be grateful for my military training with this legendary group. Between Grandad, Miss Bluebell and my future mother-in-law, I was forged in three different furnaces and I'm glad I was. Military discipline has enabled me to survive the bumpy rides of life and to enjoy the wild side to the full.

The city I liked best on this remarkable Phineas Fogg-like marathon was Amsterdam, with its bicycling population, narrow canal-side houses and red-light district, where prostitutes sat like painted dolls in amber-lit windows, giving passers-by a sample of their ingenuity. I visited the museums and Rembrandt's House, ate prodigious meals at the restaurant Smits and went home each night to a minuscule apartment in a narrow sinister street, reminding me of Jack the Ripper. The street was sinister, but nothing frightened me in those days. I was growing up in the fast lane.

My suitors in Amsterdam were all geriatric, which suited me fine. They taught me a thousand nuances of how to live life, how to present myself. They asked little in return, knowing instinctively that my innocence had already blossomed into curiosity, but that I was not yet ready to swim in deep waters. Still, they showed me what they knew about the art of entertaining a member of the opposite sex and I lapped up the lessons. We had wonderful times. They profited from my beauty, my already potent sensuality, my unusual way of viewing life and my lacerating frankness. I think I've attracted more men with that frankness and extreme talent for an insult than I have with any of my other attributes.

In Munich, I listened to the US radio programme *Luncheon in München*. There were US soldiers everywhere and three of them became my personal fans and daytime chauffeurs in a jeep. We were passing through a crowded area one day, when we saw a spectacular fight between a 6-foot 7-inch black US soldier and a 5-foot-tall local prostitute. I don't know the reason for the fight, but the girl hit him with a right uppercut worthy of Jersey Joe Walcott and, as she was around half his height, the punch landed full in the balls. He was then carried away on a stretcher to a waiting jeep.

It was in Munich that I saw men kissing each other for the first time and not only kissing. I also went with two girlfriends to the local Turkish baths and was confronted with a selection of Buddha-like, local ladies who were anxious to lose weight. Whenever I feel as if I've put on the odd kilo, I remember those Munich matrons and that stops me worrying.

It rained and rained in Munich, fine, drenching, grey

rain that seemed to make even my bones damp. Then, one day, I started to cough and the local American unit doctor, called by my three fans, said I had got pneumonia. He arranged for me to be treated at the American Base Hospital, where I lay every day in a tiny single room, swallowing pills as if my life depended on them, which maybe it did. My three drivers took me by jeep to the theatre each evening, saw the show and then drove me back to bed at the hospital.

The last city on the tour was Vienna, where just about everything happened. That year the weather was particularly hot and during the day everyone met at the Stadiumbad, just outside Vienna, where we sunbathed and had lunch. I had caught the sun as a child, but this time I turned dark brown and learned to swim, taught by an Egyptian who had won the Cross Channel race. Mistaking me, from behind, for the Austrian Olympic diving champion, he had playfully pushed me into the diving pool. As I didn't know how to swim, but had been told that you always rise to the surface three times before drowning, I stood there on the bottom, choking to death and waiting to rise. I didn't. Eventually I jumped as if on an invisible trampoline and rose to the surface. The Egyptian, who was peering into the water, wandering where I was, caught hold of my pony-tail and hauled me out. When what seemed like half a pool of water had been pumped of me, the Egyptian explained that breathing was the key to swimming and that he would teach me to swim before the next day. He did this by lowering me into the water, taking hold of my pony-tail and then calling, 'Breathe in, breathe out,' and lowering me, or lifting me, out of the water at the appropriate moment. By the next day, as he had promised, I could swim. I remember thinking about my mother who had been a fine swimmer and my aunt who had been a crawl champion. Mother had told me I was not buoyant and so I had never tried to swim.

After being photographed by the local press with three other girls, I began to receive bouquets from a man called Jurg. He was tall, blond and very handsome with that combination of decadence and discipline that fascinates women. He, too, came to the Stadiumbad once or twice, but remained aloof, watching everyone from the shelter of the bar. He invited me to go away with him for the weekend and when I said 'no' sent his girlfriend to reinforce the invitation. I said 'no' to her, too, so she arranged for all of us to have lunch together, which we did quite often. Such was my innocence, I felt reassured by her presence, though in fact they were probably waiting for me to take the bait. I never knew who this man was until many years later when I saw Brigitte Bardot in Roger Vadim's film, *And God Created Woman*. Playing opposite her was Curt Jurgens, the elegant Jurg from my days in Vienna.

A week before leaving the city, I received a touching letter from a wealthy industrialist who had followed me around the city in his car. He wrote, 'I wanted to offer you my friendship, but you don't reply to my invitations. I follow you home because I fear for your safety. You don't seem to notice the types who follow you at night. Try to learn that a friend is a very important person and if ever you need a real friend contact me.'

Conscience-stricken that I had treated him like all the other male pursuers and impressed by the dignity of the letter, I went to lunch with him and we talked for hours. I saw him again the next day and then I left Vienna. I wrote to him and he to me a couple of times a year for thirty years and we had some marvellous meetings when he sailed his yacht into the harbours of Guernsey, Malta and Palma in Majorca. He saw me grow up, marry, produce a child and write quite a few novels. He also advised me when I was at my lowest ebb at the end of my first marriage. As he had said, a friend is a very important person and he was one of the best.

CHAPTER NINE

On my return to England, I went first to see my mother. I had a suitcase full of presents for her and my father and I was thrilled at the thought of seeing them. When she opened the door, Gertrude looked at me, screamed as if she'd been struck and cried out, 'Oh God! My beautiful daughter went away and a negress returns.' Then she sobbed bitterly, pushing me away when I tried to kiss her.

I gave her her presents and told her all about the tour, wanting to take her mind off my dark brown skin, but she kept repeating, 'Why have you come home a negress?' Finally, exasperated by her histrionics, I said sharply that I remembered very well the day when I was eight, at the end of the war, when I saw a black American serviceman near the school and told half the street that there was a man painted black outside. She had taught me that the colour of his skin was perfectly normal for him, as mine was for me. I had changed in those months abroad and was now a grown woman. I felt comfortable speaking for myself after so many years of being afraid of Gertrude and I asked her therefore to remember what she'd taught me and not spoil my homecoming with recriminations about the fact that I was suntanned. After that Gertrude fell silent and sulked.

My father, when he arrived, was delightful, happy as a child with his presents and apologetic for the fact that my mother was, and in his opinion always would be, unable to accept the fact that I had grown up. I thought about this and resolved to be as reassuring as possible with Gertrude. But she glowered at me as if I were a stranger and I knew that I would leave in a few days and go to London.

I went next to see my grandparents and we had a splendid high tea on the veranda and talked about everything. When I recounted Gertrude's greeting, Nana's eyes turned steely.

'She's been impossible with your father since you went away. Bill has a lot of patience, but lately he's started going to see Reg and Marjorie. He watches television, or helps Reg in his workshop.'

Grandad got up, stretched his legs and said, 'Shall we go down to the sea, Elaine?' And we walked as we always had, Grandad talking about the past months and me picking sea-pinks. I was as happy as it's possible to be. Finally, I asked George what he thought should be done about my mother, who seemed so much worse than before I left. He shook his head, uncertain what to say.

'Nothing can be done until Gertrude wants it and she won't see a psychiatrist. In my opinion she's afraid he'll discover her secret.'

'Do you know her secret?'

'Nana thinks she does, but she has no proof, so we can't do a thing.'

I went every day to see my grandparents and also to see my aunts and Uncle Reginald, who teased me that I'd become a femme fatale. I laughed at the thought, but didn't believe a word of it. Then the tension began to increase at home, as I discovered that Gertrude was searching my belongings regularly. What was she looking for? I could never understand. Finally I decided to go to London. I'd expected Gertrude to be happy to see me home and was bitterly disappointed by the violence of her reactions. When the local paper photographed me, Gertrude sat staring at the picture and muttering, 'She's ugly now and black.'

I took a service flat in one of the narrow streets near Harrods and, as I was frozen, went by bus to Liberty's, always one of my favourite stores, to buy a pullover. I was debating what colour to choose, when I heard a voice that I hadn't forgotten.

'I see you've not lost those magnificent tits.'

Turning, I saw Jess Yates hurrying towards me, beaming

with delight. 'We'll go to lunch,' he said, guiding me to a Greek café, where he ordered a fry-up of just about everything and doused the plate liberally with HP sauce.

After counts in Bavaria, bankers in Brussels and the millionaire in Vienna, Jess seemed like a breath of fresh air. He was dressed by Gieves & Hawkes of Savile Row and looked well, apart from his hair, which frizzed so hard it formed a halo around his plate face, like a pre-Raphaelite hero. I suggested a haircut.

'No,' he replied, 'my mother likes to do it.'

'When did she do it last?' I asked.

'At Christmas,' he said.

It was now October. I also noticed that Jess seemed to be suffocating in a collar that pinched his neck in a noose-like grip.

'Your collar's too tight,' I said.

'Nonsense, I take a 14½ collar, always have done.'

Jess weighed a good 15½ stone at the time and I thought he needed a 16½ collar.

'It's too tight,' I said.

'My mother buys my size and that's that,' he snapped.

After lunch, I led Jess back to the men's section of Liberty's and asked for his neck to be measured. The salesman said he needed a good 16½. Jess was speechless for two seconds. 'I thought my collars felt a bit tight lately,' he said, shaking his head in perplexity.

The salesman looked askance and, to avoid further useless conversation, I suggested that Jess buy some new shirts. Then we went to the pictures. I can't remember the film, but it was funny and we laughed loud and long together. Jess had an apartment in Maida Vale at the time and he invited me to lunch there the following Sunday. I accepted, amused, when he walked away muttering to himself, 'I don't know what my mother's going to say when she finds out that I take a size 16½ collar. When I was fourteen I took a 14½. She won't be pleased that someone noticed that! She'll ask who it was!!'

The following Sunday, I arrived at the block where Jess lived and found him listening to an Edith Piaf record and searching for a lost letter. The room was littered with papers and mountains of books and records. Piaf's impressive voice sang 'Non, je regretted rien' and I hoped I wouldn't regret coming to see him. I didn't. We ate lunch in a café round the corner, Jess ordering bacon and eggs and fried bread and chips and sausages and the bottle of HP sauce. Then we went into town and walked in the park, talking about everything, particularly his work at the BBC. Jess reminisced about the war and his days in the Pay Corps. As he was unable, even on pain of death, to add two plus two, I never worked out why Jess was put in the Pay Corps. But he was and the experience nearly provoked a breakdown. Surrounded by papers needing dexterity with figures, he became submerged and resolved the problem by sending all the papers to British Army HQ in Jerusalem, or perhaps it was Damascus, I've forgotten. Then he got out his camera and took photographs of the colonel of the regiment and his family and all the officers and then all the men. When the war ended, he was making a lot of money on the vanity of others.

In the early evening, Jess took me back to my service flat and we arranged to meet again the following day. As I didn't know London, he drew a map of the fish restaurant where we would be eating. His way of marking reference points on maps was always the nearest public lavatory. 'Turn right at the public lavatory' was his catch-phrase. When I direct someone, it's always via the Royal Academy, Foyles, the British Museum, or Marble Arch. Another of my friends in London directs his friends by restaurants. To each his priority.

Jess arrived an hour late for the date. I was seething with anger and was hard pressed not to sock him in the eye. As I'm always on time, it took a miracle for me to learn that Jess never knew what day or hour it was and that 60 minutes late was almost on time for him, two or three hours being par for the course. When I snapped at him, Jess laughed like a child. 'You look wonderful when you're angry, like Joan Crawford only better.' Then he ordered fillet of halibut with chips and HP sauce. After the meal, we went to the Odeon in Leicester Square, where Jess regaled me with stories of his early days when he had played the organ in cinemas throughout Britain, popping up out of a hole in the ground on the Mighty Wurlitzer and occasionally singing in the high-pitched voice he called tenor and I falsetto, to his intense chagrin.

Sometimes, we sang improvised duets, laughing at Jess' warbling high notes and my desire to begin all the melodies well below middle C. Jess was the funniest man I had ever met, either before or since, and even now, there are times when I remember with pleasure the most outrageous explosions of laughter that punctuated our courtship and marriage.

There are those in my family who remember sadness, being abandoned, persecuted or ill-treated. My mother was the champion, hands down, at these memories, all of them lies. I've learned to remember the positive and bury most of the negative and the tragic below sea level. No one forgets, but sometimes it's better to remember the funny moments, the golden days of loving and sharing than the times when everything turned sombre and we wondered if we'd ever be happy again.

Jess and I met often from that day onwards. A month later, he suggested dinner along the block from where he lived. After dinner, he suggested bed and I thought, well, it's time and followed him to the apartment. It seemed meant to be and I was not afraid of what to me was hitherto unknown. In the bedroom, Jess became supersonic, throwing off his clothes and putting his fingers through three condoms in his excitement. Even pre-coital, he made me laugh! The event passed without problem, except that at one point Jess asked me where my left leg was and we discovered it was wrapped round the back of his neck and had knocked off his glasses. The only other problem was that I, not realising that men need a rest afterwards, wanted to do it all again immediately and then again, and again. At two in the morning, Jess put me in the spare bed in the living room and retired behind locked doors to recover.

Alone, I went over what had happened, thrilled by this new occupation that seemed like the panacea for all ills. Unable to sleep, I rose at six-thirty and stared out of the window. There was nothing to see but an inner well or courtyard and so I put a record on Jess' record player. It was one of his favourite singers, Julie London and the song was 'Oh, Do it Again'. While she sang provocatively, Jess called out from his room. 'I'm coming out in five minutes and we'll have breakfast and no I can't do it again!'

From that day onwards, we met almost daily. We roamed Portobello Market, ate at Jess' favourite fry-up cafés, or at Blooms and Isow's, where I liked the food. We went to the ballet, the Design Centre and saw innumerable films, including Greta Garbo in *Anna Karenina*, a film that made Jess and all the men in the audience cry. Garbo's magic was potent and Jess had lived every second of cinematic magic. He always did. When we went to see *Ben Hur*, he was out of breath and exhausted for hours because of 'having driven in that bloody chariot race'! I returned home for Christmas, disappointed to find Gertrude as hostile as ever and given to searching my baggage every few minutes. Over Christmas Eve dinner, she asked if it was true that I'd been seen with Jess Yates. I said yes he was a good friend.

'He's disgusting,' hissed my mother. 'I don't want you to be seen with him. He has a reputation for running after women.'

Christmas was strained because of her criticisms of Jess and her attacks on me, which were even more vitriolic. My principal sins were the fact that my eyes looked greener and my hair was getting straighter. At that time, I had a less wavy but still permed hairdo. I have the world's straightest hair and dreamed at this time of letting it hang down as it wanted to. My mother considered straight hair the territory of degenerates and bone-idle people. Her continual haranguing for days on end saddened me, making me remember the tensions of my childhood. My father was ill at this time with what later turned out to be a brain tumour and I left him in peace, not mentioning Gertrude's incessant complaining. But at mealtimes, when he joined us, she spewed revenge, hate and rancour and Bill and I looked at each other across the table, as we always had, resigned, not knowing what to do. We were sad, but we were also tired of her.

I was glad to return to London. On the train, I remember wondering how to handle future relations with Gertrude. I loved her and needed her support, but her view of life and people was twisted and she resented everyone with whom I came into contact and always had. Worse, she particularly hated Nana, because of her bitter jealousy of Constance's charm and wonderful cooking that she took as a personal criticism, my aunts and now Jess. I was too young to understand fully that my mother viewed life through a dark, cracked mirror. Perhaps in her early teens, she had been gay and full of hope, but by the age of twenty-five, she was already full of tranquillisers and sleeping more than half of each day. As the train pulled into Euston, I saw Jess on the platform with a giant bunch of flowers in his hand wearing a hat that was too small for his head. His face lit with pleasure and he talked non-stop, as he always did when euphoric. I was as euphoric as he and felt suddenly as if I belonged.

We ate dinner together and then spent the New Year weekend at Jess' apartment. I was as happy was any young girl could be and Jess was happy, too. Far away from the pressure of our mothers, we did what all couples do, sharing favourite pursuits, planning the months ahead, window shopping at night, laughing at private jokes and establishing routines that were precious to both of us.

On New Year's Eve, Jess ordered a delicious dinner and for once forgot the HP sauce. Afterwards, we returned to his apartment and as midnight struck he said, 'Now you can propose to me.'

I stared at him, uncertain what to say.

Jess explained, 'I can't propose to you because my mother will kill me if I do, so you propose to me and I'll say yes.'

Having had vast experience of a difficult mother, I was sympathetic and proposed to him and Jess said, 'Yes,' tears of emotion in his eyes. Then we went to bed and slept like logs.

The wedding was fixed for the month of June. In April, Jess was due to return to the north Wales resort of Llandudno, where his family lived, to help organise it. The season was about to begin in a newly acquired hotel that had taken his mother's eye and Jess had agreed to manage it. I would do three months as a replacement for a girl who had left a London revue and then travel to Wales and stay in the hotel for the three weeks before the wedding. We would return to London, Jess told me, at the end of the season. We both decided to say nothing of our plans to my mother at least for the moment.

Jess ordered a new suit for the wedding. He loved new clothes and, as his mother always paid for them, was often given to scouting around Simpson's and Savile Row. He had a habit of putting the trousers of one suit with the jacket of another, giving him an absent-minded air, but it was all part of the unique character of the man. I even liked the fact that putting two shoes on of the same pair was quite a problem for Jess, who talked so much, he simply put on whatever came to hand first. I used to think about him for hours, laughing joyfully at his funny ways, his outrageous exaggerations and his abominable habit of putting his foot out when someone ran by, tripping them up. His other pet joke was slipping friends, enemies and family powerful doses of laxative. He once gave me thirty leaves of senna infused overnight 'to cure your toothache'. I drank it all. Then, later in the day, I went to the Savoy Hotel to welcome some American friends who were visiting London. The senna hit me just at the moment when the darling doorman of the Savoy opened the door of the taxi for me. He was then confronted by an elegantly dressed young woman, who suddenly ran like Zatopek through the entrance doors of the hotel, veering left to the toilets like a human Ferrari. It says a great deal for the power of my sphincter muscle that I managed to get there, to say nothing of the power of the senna tea! I was very annoyed with Jess about this near accident at the Savoy and bellowed like Raging Bull. But he laughed so hard I ended up laughing with him. There was nothing in the world I liked better at that time than laughing with Jess. I was blind to the fact that, at nearly forty, he remained, like Peter Pan, the eternal child.

London without Jess was lonely. I wrote to him and to my mother, who continued with her lists of criticisms. When I finally told her I was going to marry Jess, she threatened to go to court to stop me. I ceased contact for a while.

Before he left London, Jess had been traumatised by the break-up of one of his friend's marriages. The man had been considerably older than his wife, who had known only her husband before running off with a seductive actor. Jess decided I should get experience before I got married, so I wouldn't 'get curious' about men afterwards. If I had been a little more worldly, I might have been worried by his final instruction: 'Write and tell me all about your boyfriends, won't you.'

One evening, I was entering the theatre when a handsome man said, 'Hello, I've been waiting ages to meet you. My name's Donald Campbell.' He was a wonderfully charming character with impeccable manners and a gull-winged Mercedes that gave me claustrophobia when he drove me up Park Lane at 120 mph. His boyish pleasure in speed, women, laughter and friends was infectious and I saw him a few times for lunch at the fashionable restaurant Rules and for fun here and there. He liked fun with a capital F and so did I. But our relationship was brief and, adorable as he was in bed, I really didn't care too much for being driven at 120 mph in the centre of London, so we remained friends, but not driving ones.

When I heard what had happened to him at Coniston Water in the Lake District, after his world record attempt, I was immensely saddened. I remember him as a man who surrounded himself with beautiful things and who loved the intoxicating atmosphere of risk. He was human but never ordinary, hedonistic but never shallow. Finally, I went to Euston and took the train to Wales, accompanied by two trunks and full of every great expectation known to man. When I arrived at Deganwy Station, I was met by Jess and the station master, who stared at me as if I were a Martian and said in a wonderful Welsh accent. 'Oo... ah... eh... we've never had anyone like you here!'

Jess rushed me to the hotel. 'We're going to meet my mother and brother and friends in an hour, get ready and look beautiful.'

I later walked into a room where I was presented to Edward Yates, a dear man and a war hero, who was as truthful and honourable as Jess was not. Then Jess led me to meet a white-haired lady in a very smart navy blue ensemble. He said, 'Mother, this is Elaine. Elaine meet my mother.'

I held out my hand. Sybil Yates ignored it and said, 'There are three kinds of folk I don't like to have in my hotel: Jews, Catholics and theatricals.' And with that welcome she turned to Jess and I turned my back on her.

I was anguished in the extreme, but did my best to hold my head high. Teddy Yates handed me a glass of orange juice and said, 'You've gone a bit pale.' I smiled and so did he and it gave me the courage to face the curious future that was, for nearly twenty years, my destiny. I should have run a mile, but I didn't. In my family we stand firm.

PART TWO

THE MARRIED YEARS – JESS YATES' MARIONETTE

'Those who know don't talk and those who talk don't know.'

JAPANESE PROVERB

CHAPTER TEN

On the morning of the wedding, my mother howled in anguish, 'She's no right to get married. She belongs to me. She must come home and live with me. She's mine.'

Guests looking on in the dining room of Jess' family hotel stared askance at the distraught woman in the slate-grey lace suit. Luigi, the Italian dessert chef, was so unnerved by Gertrude's histrionics that he put salt instead of sugar in the butter icing of the cake that the wedding party was to consume at lunch after the ceremony.

On many of the wedding photographs, Jess is linking arms with his mother and smiling at camera. I'm standing alone, holding my bouquet of roses and stephanotis, with a wry smile on my face. I was wondering what to do with a husband who seemed to think he'd just married his mum. I remembered the reaction of his friends when he told them we were going to be married: astonishment, belated congratulations, then, from each and every one, 'Does your mother know, Jess? Are you sure she'll let you get married?' As Jess was heading for his fortieth birthday, I had laughed at their consternation. I was wrong to have done so.

Knowing we would have trouble with my mother, we had wisely limited the invitations to family and two friends of my future mother-in-law. I wore ice pink, with transparent shoes from Ernest Chaussures in Paris, the greatest shoe shop I have ever been to. (All the naughty girls – and the boy-girls – of Pigalle bought their shoes at Ernest Chaussures.) The bouquet was wired to fall in a certain way down the centre of my skirt. I didn't realise it, but the shoes and bouquet were a bit before their time. When Paula found the shoes twenty years later, she said, 'Those shoes you wore for your wedding are coming into fashion Mummy.'

After a catastrophic wedding breakfast, when the salt-instead-of-sugar icing made certain guests heave, Jess and I drove off on honeymoon to Clough Williams-Ellis' fabulous folly, Portmeirion, in Penrhyndeudraeth. On arrival, we were welcomed by Michael Trevor Williams, a highly amusing, erudite and elegant character, who showed us around the main building, before taking us to our 'cottage' in Fountain Court. It was a sunny day and the buildings of the village were golden in the summer light. I was as happy as a child, until I noticed that Jess had suddenly turned very pale.

When I had unpacked, I took a shower and Jess said he was going to call his mother. I was stepping out of the shower when I heard him, obviously distressed, talking to Sybil.

'What am I going to do, Mother, there's a huge pool outside the window. I nearly fainted when I saw it. Can I come home? What? But you know I can't stand the sight of water... Can I come home Mother...? Are you there...? Are you there...? Oh God! She's hung up.'

I stood in the bathroom, staring at my reflection in the mirror. Imagine! Jess asking to go home when he had only just arrived. Half of me wanted to laugh and half to cry. Finally, I returned to the main room and suggested we look around the village. Jess closed his eyes on passing the pool and I thought how his terror of water and my passion for it were the first indication of our very different natures. For the moment, I tried not to worry about my husband's pasty face and trembling hands. Then I remembered Grandad's strange comment when I had asked him what he thought of Jess. George had looked out over the Conway estuary and said softy, 'I learned when I was very young that you never know a man until you've been back to the wall with him.' In those days young girls knew little of psychology and I had thought George was just being a bit strange. I should have known better and, as I write these memoirs, I realise that I married, thinking, or perhaps hoping, that most men were like George and marriages were for ever. For me, married couples didn't lie to each other. They just worked together to a common destiny. It was an idealistic thought, but a mistaken one.

After a lovely dinner and a stroll in the moonlight, we slept like logs as it had been such a tiring day. The following morning, we went to Blackrock Sands and I danced on the beach from sheer happiness. Then I forgot to put my shoes back on and returned barefoot to the hotel. Jess sidled close to the wall, eyes shut as he passed the dreaded pool, but he liked the suite very much for its view of the estuary. I liked the seabirds wheeling overhead and making love to my husband, so he could forget water, pools and anything else that bothered him.

Three days later, we returned to the hotel bought by Sybil because she had loved the stylish old building and had paid little for it. It was losing money and in danger of bankruptcy. Sybil was sure she could put it back on its feet again with Jess to manage and do all the publicity photographs. While Jess ran the new place, she and Teddy would continue with her other hotel in nearby Llandudno. Jess had omitted to tell me of this arrangement and I still thought we were going back to London in October. I was so upset by this. It had never been my ambition to run a hotel, and I felt that I was losing control of my life.

Our quarters in the hotel comprised the former playroom and a bathroom. The well-named playroom was enormous and full of Jess' things that had been sent from

London. At one end of the room there was a cathedral-like bed that he had bought in an auction at a stately home, specially for his conjugal antics. We wanted a child as quickly as possible because of the age difference of almost twenty years, so we applied ourselves to long, erotic sessions with ever-increasing regularity. The antique bed broke after ten days and its replacement four weeks later! Then Jess read in one of his collection of pornographic magazines (numbering about 700 and kept in piles under the bed in case his mother searched the room) that it was possible to achieve maximum penetration while swinging from a trapeze-like contrivance in the general direction of the person on the bed. I got worried at this point in case I ended up with two navels, two vaginas or worse, but Jess wanted to try. He rigged up a swinging seat from a hook in the ceiling and proceeded to practise the run-up to intercourse. Unfortunately, he got so excited he swung too far and was suddenly projected a good 6 feet up in the air and 10 feet away from me. The hook in the ceiling broke, bringing down part of the ceiling and three floorboards caved inwards as Jess' 16 stone fell like a meteorite on to the worm-eaten wood.

The doctor was called and came at once, despite the hour. He took one look at the naked Jess sitting on the floor with one foot stuck between the floorboards of the ceiling and me, naked in bed, laughing hysterically at the bewildered look on my husband's face. If the doctor understood what had happened, he never mentioned the incident again and after prescribing a sedative for Jess, whose blood pressure had shot through the ceiling when his foot went through the floor, he left us.

Jess was distraught, worrying how to tell his mother about the hole in the floor and the caved-in roof. I reassured him as best I was able and rang for an early breakfast. Face to face with a giant tray of bacon, eggs, black pudding, sausages and mushrooms, plus the obligatory bottle of HP sauce, Jess cheered up, at least for a few minutes. Then the eighty-five-year-old housekeeper of the hotel appeared and spoke with great solemnity: 'Mr Yates, beds broken, the ceiling brought down and floorboards shattered. We have never had such happenings in the hotel. The staff are gossiping in a most unseemly fashion. It will cause tongues to wag in the village, that's for sure.'

And it did!

It was an explosive start to the marriage and the laughter and tears that followed were often provoked by Jess' sexual fantasies, his fears, his desire to be Casanova, Al Capone and Ali Khan and his realisation that sometimes thinking about things is easier and safer than doing them, at least when you weigh 16 stone.

CHAPTER ELEVEN

Our return from honeymoon was memorable because of Jess' acrobatics in the playroom. I loved to laugh and he was a naturally funny man. In fact, he was like the little girl in the rhyme we learn as children – 'When he was good he was very very good and when he was bad he was horrid.'

In that period, his mother was always awful. When I failed to receive letters from my family and friends, I asked the receptionist if I had had any since I was married. 'Yes,' she replied, blushing furiously, 'your mother-in-law took them all.'

When Sybil arrived, I asked if I could have my letters. She looked straight through me and said, 'I'm the only Mrs Yates here and any letter sent in that name is mine.'

With that, she left me and returned to the other hotel in Llandudno. I wrote and asked my friends and family to write to me in my maiden name.

I was then told by Jess that I must stay in our suite and not come downstairs, because his mother didn't wish me to have anything to do with the hotel. I said nothing, but I cried enough for six, because I had no idea what to do about the hostility of the most important person in Jess' life. I wanted to get on with Sybil, but she was a fiercely possessive woman who would never let go of her son.

My mother wrote offensive letters at least twice a week and, as the hotel was only ninety miles from her home, often arrived to see us, with or without my father. She was always aggressive and given to following Jess around the hotel, spying on him in case he threw a chambermaid or two into bed. He didn't, but Gertrude was sure he would, some day.

Then something difficult happened, the first of three upsetting things that caused ructions between Jess and his mother and me.

Jess had taken publicity photos for the next year's brochure of the hotel and over afternoon tea in the private lounge showed them to Sybil, Teddy and me. They were beautiful, but on the pictures of the exterior there was no trace of the railway line that ran immediately next to the River Wing of the hotel. When I said, 'The shots are all marvellous, but cheating on the exterior shots could give you problems. Some people don't like the trains passing at five-thirty in the morning,' Jess blustered. Sybil glowered, but Teddy said, 'Best do those again Jess. We don't want folk walking out. It's best that they know exactly what the hotel is like.'

A row followed, with Jess accusing me of causing problems. Sybil stayed silent, because she knew I was right. Teddy got up and walked out. It might have seemed like a minor confrontation, but it would prove to be a watershed in our marriage.

The second incident concerned the nocturnal departure of the chef and his second-in-command just before the Bank Holiday. I was up and almost dressed when a young waitress hammered at the door. I opened it and she cried out, 'Chef's gone in the night, madam.'

I replied, 'Ask the second to do the breakfast.'

'He's gone, too, madam, and your husband's had a panic attack and gone home to his mother. Can you come? There are seventy-six guests waiting for their breakfast.'

I can still remember the terror that took hold of me at that moment. Seventy-six people waiting for their breakfast and I couldn't boil water. I'd learned Latin and maths and all manner of erudite pursuits, but I couldn't cook. Still, something had to be done, so I hurried to the kitchen with a look of confidence I was far from feeling. Utterly petrified, I told the waiters to apologise to the guests for the 'accident' that necessitated the cancellation of everything on the breakfast menu except scrambled eggs. I'd seen my nana make those once or twice and hoped I could remember how.

The ballet of breakfast began, with coffee and tea made by the stillroom maid, who also did the toast, while an aged Irish cleaner and I turned out mountains of scrambled eggs. I trembled so hard and felt so sick that I needed a miracle to keep upright.

Teddy arrived before the end of breakfast and when he took over, I rushed upstairs to telephone my mother-in-law to inform her that the chef wouldn't be back. Then I sat on my bed and cried and cried and cried. I had left home in my teens to travel around Europe, follow a physically gruelling regime and had also had to cope with two hostile matriarchs. I felt alone, worried that my marriage to Jess was taking a turn for the worse and I didn't want to live in an hotel. I couldn't cook and hated having to be sociable with people I had never met before. I wanted to be secure in the silence of my room, but it was no longer possible.

When Teddy appeared, he looked at my eyes swollen with tears and said, 'I think you and I had best take the hoteliers' special emergency cookery course this winter, Elaine. Then, if this happens again, either here or at the other hotel, we'll be prepared.'

And that was what we did. He was a remarkable man, a former lieutenant commander in the Royal Navy and the object of all Jess' jealousy. He once witnessed Jess in a terrible rage, when he had written something for a friend to say in a speech and had signed the speech for publication with the name Jess Yates. The content of the speech was 90 per cent Oscar Wilde and I said, 'You can't sign it with your name when Wilde wrote most of it.'

'How did you know?' he replied. 'You and your fucking brain will end this marriage.'

Jess shouted the odds for five minutes, until suddenly, Teddy, normally so polite and placid said, 'You must start to realise Jess that not everyone in the world is as ill-educated as you, nor as pathological a liar.' And with that he went home. Jess couldn't believe it and sat down, stunned, in his favourite armchair. 'My brother has never said anything like that before.' And I replied, 'Teddy's trying to stop you making trouble for yourself. Listen to him.'

But Jess never did. Cheating, lying and making folk believe what he said, were his way of proving himself top dog. I don't know what caused it, perhaps problems at school. I never found out.

One August Bank Holiday Saturday, the hotel staff, led by a German waitress, demanded double wages for the rest of the season or they would leave. 'You deal with that,' Jess said, 'I'm going home to my mother for a day or two.'

I telephoned Jess' brother to ask if we could augment the salaries in view of the threat.

'Not a penny,' he replied.

A few minutes later the girl came to see me. 'Well, have you decided what to do?'

As I had no choice in the matter, I replied that I had decided to let everyone go. I asked that they vacate the hotel immediately and they did, leaving us staffed by two barmen, our elderly housekeeper and the new chef and his second. About the only thing that kept me going at this time was the thought of returning to London at the end of the season and being happy and alone with Jess, as we had once before. I was still unaware that other plans had been made for our future.

By mid August I began to fall asleep all the time and, wondering if I were anaemic, went to see the doctor. I was told that the resident doctor would return at the end of the school holidays. The locum gave me some vitamin C tablets and told me to return in the first week in September. When I did, and after an examination, I was told that my baby would arrive in April. I had thought the stress of the two mothers' jealousy and the constant problems in the hotel had disrupted my menstrual cycle. I was wrong and delighted to be so. I ran all the way back to the hotel, singing like Nellie Melba and leaping up in the air in impromptu entrechats.

Jess was in the garden when I arrived and I told him the news. He was as joyful as I and we ran to the hotel to telephone his family and to talk about our son arriving. From the first, I was convinced that I would have a boy, but again, I was wrong and didn't mind at all. Jess' brother was as happy as a child, but Sybil refused to believe that this glamorous creature could have a baby. When I was seven months' pregnant and still wearing my normal clothes, Sybil introduced me to her friend saying, 'This is Elaine, my daughter-in-law, who thinks she is pregnant.' I changed shape radically a couple of weeks later.

One day, I asked Jess exactly when we would be returning to London.

'Never,' he replied. 'I've come here to be near my mother and here I'll stay.'

Seeing my stricken face, he howled with laughter and said a favourite phrase of his that was to run like a leitmotif through our marriage. 'Despite your fabulous brain you believe everything I say. You've no idea when I lie have you? That shows that even great brains can be as stupid as mules.'

I cried and cried and couldn't stop crying. The more I cried, the more Jess laughed, until he almost lost control. In the five years that I lived in the hotel I rarely got through a day without crying for hours on end. I had been brought up to believe in the truth and now it dawned on me that for Jess the truth was something to be avoided at all costs. I felt as if I were living on quicksand and very soon became disillusioned. When I tried to analyse Jess' need to lie, I couldn't. It wasn't always to make himself look grand, or to get out of trouble. If I asked what he ate for breakfast on days when I was too busy to eat with him, he would say bacon and eggs. In fact, he had had kippers. In other words, it seemed to me that he lied for the sheer love of lying. This was strange, because for all her faults, my mother-in-law was honest and capable of being frank and Jess' brother, Teddy, was an honourable man for whom lies were anathema.

Realising after some time that he had seriously upset me, Jess turned on the full heat of his charm and organised an exceptional Christmas for us. At New Year, my mother sent some of the most injurious letters I'd ever read on the subject of Jess. These were read first by my mother-in-law, who still managed to intercept and read all my mail, and then by Jess, to whom she passed them on and who finally gave them to me. My mother-in-law never spoke to Gertrude again. Jess pretended friendship but hated her and plotted revenge. It was the only thing they had in common, a veritable passion for revenge. Jess spent most of his afternoons plotting the dire things he would do to those he disliked.

When the date came for Paula's arrival, the doctor had to go away for forty-eight hours. He asked me to go into the nursing home 'just in case'. Nothing happened during that time. Then, seeing that I was feeling a bit ill, a nurse asked me if I was in labour. 'I don't know,' I replied. In those days, the preparation of pregnant women was either absent, or perfunctory, and I had no idea how giving birth would feel. I had just read Grantley Dick Read's book *Painless Childbirth* and wanted more than anything to relax and let the baby arrive without squashing its head so it became lopsided like that of the Parisian millionaire in what now seemed like my distant past. It had taken four months to learn the technique. It was a huge help as I was able to float off to another place during labour when the pain got too much.

Paula arrived at twenty minutes after midnight on 24 April 1959. I had started labour at seven the previous evening and not liking too much the backache and nausea had decided to put mind over matter and sleep. I woke at midnight with the peculiar feeling of wanting to push. A nurse came in, then ran out and hared down the corridor. Minutes later, the doctor arrived wearing his trousers and a pyjama jacket. All I can remember is his saying, 'Elaine, when I tell you to stop pushing, for God's sake STOP.'

I stopped when the baby was there. It was, and remains, the best moment of my life and I loved Paula with all my heart. In the days following, Jess kept coming to see the baby and to exhort me to come back to the hotel, where he didn't know how to do the bookkeeping, nor the PAYE for the staff. Despite his need, a painful mastitis kept me in bed for a while, being pumped by the nurses, as if I were a gift from the Milk Marketing Board. I had also had a serious loss of vision, which worried me to death. My sight improved after six months, but never returned to how it had been before.

I chose Paula's name and Jess chose the second name, the Queen's, which I found too conventional, but said nothing as I'd been allowed first choice. She was christened Paula Elizabeth Yates in Llandudno and from that moment on my life took an upturn, at least for a while.

I was totally happy with my baby, but often shocked by the reactions of certain people. When I walked Paula in her pram near the sea one day, a woman stopped, looked and then said, 'What a beautiful child, who does it belong to?'

'It's my daughter,' I replied, nearly bursting with pride.

'Yours!' she said. 'Have you had a child?'

This conversation was often repeated and always upset me. I was immensely proud of my daughter and proud, too, that I had given birth to this precious, wonderful little girl. I felt as if I were only half human in their eyes, yet I'm very human indeed. I got the same reaction when I said that I didn't smoke or drink. This was greeted with incredulity or disbelief. I think that young women with red hair, hourglass figures and wilful natures upset a great many people. They fall into a stereotype and are expected to spit on floors, smoke like chimneys and drink whisky on the rocks. I'm lucky that I never started smoking – I remember the terrible shock I had when my mother began to smoke at the age of fifty-five and, given her addictive personality, smoked three packs a day, making her house resemble Manchester in a pea-soup fog.

As the new season approached, Jess became tense and silent. Knowing that he had cheated on the brochure photographs, he was running scared. He had not dared tell anyone that he had ordered the printing of the brochures without changing the exteriors. Jess' panicky state changed our life together, too. He was irritable and silent, sitting with hunched shoulders and hating every moment spent in the hotel. In the first year of our marriage, we had never stopped making love in order to have a child. Now we rarely started. I hoped it was a phase that would pass. But either Jess locked himself in his room, or disappeared to his mother's house, so that he wouldn't have to face guests who demanded to see the manager so that he could show them how he had avoided the railway line on the photographs in their brochure!

It was at this time that a third grave problem arose that changed our everyday existence. Jess developed stink. 'Stink' was my name for this mysterious condition, which we both treated as if it were an enemy that had invaded his body. It was not a bowel or bladder smell, simply a terrible, sickly catastrophe of an odour that rose from his body like mist from a marsh. I saw it as an animalistic reaction to terror and wondered if it would ever go away. The doctor was puzzled. Jess' mother breathed hard, but didn't know what to say. Neither did I.

The light relief in certain difficult periods of my first marriage came from unexpected sources. One was my habit of practising changing gear in the car on Jess' willy. Unaware that I was a born left-hander, I had a lot of difficulty during my driving lessons, with the marvellously patient, ex-Inspector Idris Evans, in working out which way was third gear and which way was top gear. Jess adored my pre-driving test practice sessions that always ended in the same way: first gear, second gear... up and over... third gear, top... oh... ah... oooooooooohhhhhhhh. Do it again Elaine!

I didn't want to cause ripples in our marriage by dwelling on the bad times with Jess. My childhood had been very tough, but it prepared me for what I thought were maybe the normal travails of marriage – divorce was still taboo and people simply didn't talk about their relationship problems. When you love someone, it is so very difficult to think of them objectively, dispassionately, and I felt a strong urge to protect Jess, even when he acted abominably towards me.

In view of the 'stink' problem, I did my best to learn from Sybil and Teddy how to manage the daily routines of the hotel – how to check the kitchen orders, how to do the bookkeeping and so on. Teddy ordered for the four bars, with their capacity for over 500 people. I even tried to learn that. Above all, I had to learn how to handle the creditors who often formed lines near the reception desk. They were all very kind to me and I remember them with gratitude. They probably realised that I was as upset as they were about the hotel's debts. I told them the truth, sometimes promising money in a few days when it was available. For their part, they gave us bar umbrellas and, for a long time, their patience.

After the débâcle of the walk-out of the professional hotel staff the previous summer, I had decided to use students from Bangor and Liverpool Universities. They were put on end-of-season bonus schemes and all wanted to earn as much money as possible. They were intelligent, kind, cheerful and fun. The few exceptions included a young man who made off with certain contents of the wine cellar and another who informed me that he would prefer my job to his as barman, 'Because I am exhausted by the hours, madam.' I immediately offered to take his job and for him to take mine and gave him a list of my duties, which started at five in the morning – 'Wake up and check of the staff' – and ended between midnight and one a.m. when I finished checking the books. He lasted two days before asking to return to the bar. This was the same young man who punched Jess in the eye when he was wearing his glasses, which broke, cutting his upper eyelid. At that point, Chef Fox, from Cheshire who was at the kitchen hot plate, leaped over in order to go to Jess' assistance, got stuck halfway over and collapsed on to the hot plate, severely roasting his balls. He was such a kind man and a chef of the old style. I hope that he and his balls are still going strong!

One of the students who came to work for us asked me if he could sing in the bar to earn more money. I auditioned him, thought his voice marvellous and put him on that the same night. He was a riotous success from the start and later found fame as the folk singer Roger Whittaker.

Suspecting both mental and physical illness, Teddy asked Jess to make a will. Jess' blood pressure had risen as high as Everest and his mother and brother both felt he should 'put his affairs in order'. I asked that the will be in Paula's favour, not mine. Jess immediately became hysterical, ran blindly to the front door of the hotel with his arms outstretched and, because of the force of his weight and the speed of his flight, put his hand through the plate-glass door panel. He severed an artery, blood shot all over the entrance to the hotel and Jess sobbed and screamed, 'I'll never make a will, never, because the day I do, I'll die like my father.'

His father had died when Jess was an adolescent. He was not old, perhaps in his forties or fifties. Later, a fortune teller had predicted that Jess would die like his father, having just made his will. Teddy shook his head in despair. Even Sybil was outraged by the event. Guests stared in horror at the blood and our family doctor arrived, looked hard at Jess and then led him away to have his hand stitched. When it was done, the doctor told me, 'If he continues like this, he'll have to see a psychiatrist. It isn't normal behaviour for an adult and he seems to be getting worse.'

I said nothing at all, because suddenly I felt lost, unable to work out what to say or do, except put on a brave face and a smile when I was with friends and visitors.

At the end of the season, with the accountants shaking their heads over the hotel results, Jess told me he had put ads in various papers to find girls willing to pose for 'pin-up pictures' which he could then sell to saucy magazines. 'It'll save the hotel from bankruptcy,' he said.

He sent me to choose the prettiest of the applicants and, like a fool, I believed every word and went. Jess was a wonderful photographer and I was sure he could make money. He had photographed the great and the famous and I had rarely seen a bad result. I went willingly and chose from the applicants.

In June, my parents came to stay for their holidays. Jess had prepared a famous tape, pirated by staff of the BBC, to play for my mother. The tape began like an outside broadcast, with a typical commentator announcing the annual 'Crepitating Contest'. Gertrude listened, thinking it was a sporting broadcast. When she finally registered the giant farts of that legendary tape of the 'Farting Contest', she laughed so much she had to go to her room to recover. Ever darker, Jess was disappointed that she hadn't taken offence and gone home. Yet he talked for days about his discovery that Gertrude could laugh!

Gertrude and Bill were not indulgent grandparents – I can't remember when my mum spent any quality time with Paula. It was at this time we'd been told that Dad was also suffering from Parkinsons.

In the second week of her stay, my mother fled the hotel screaming for all to hear, 'That monster is making pornographic films. I'll have him arrested.' My father, white faced and trembling with rage, followed her to the station at the bottom of the garden and I ran after them, asking Bill what had happened.

'I can't discuss it,' he said. 'I shall never come here again Elaine. I wish you luck but I fear you'll have to leave that man. He's playing you for a fool.'

It was one thing for my mother, who was often hysterical, to leave, but that my father wouldn't explain was awful. I went back to the hotel and up to the playroom, which had once been our bedroom but, since our move to a three-room suite, had become Jess' photographic studio. When I tried the door, it was locked. I knocked. Jess asked me to return in half an hour. He was marvellously convincing, explaining that he'd been photographing two girls in the near nude when my mother had walked in and, given her complexes about sex, had thought he was making pornographic films. I accepted the explanation, knowing Gertrude's capacity for hating anything to do with sex or nudity. Perhaps I wanted to believe Jess, or perhaps, as he so often said, I was incapable of understanding that he lied. I was gullible, vulnerable and out of my depth.

The matter came to a head six months later when I, thinking that Jess was in the wine cellar with his brother, gave a visiting woman friend a tour of the hotel, ending it at the playroom, so that I could show her the hole in the ceiling. We walked in together and came to a halt before Jess filming what was indisputably pornographic material, girls masturbating, lesbian love et cetera. Stunned, I went with my friend to the garden and sat in silence. Instead of sobbing, as I usually did, I battled with a white-hot rage. After a few seconds I ran back to the playroom, threw Jess and the two girls out, hurled his 16-mm camera through the window and then broke up the set of a little bedroom where they had been working. Jess turned and began to run towards the stairway. I followed roaring with rage and doing a good imitation of Genghis Khan. Jess escaped to the safety of his mother's place, where he stayed for some days.

The testing time had come again and I didn't feel up to it, but I had a child who needed me and, despite everything, I knew Jess needed me, too. I was still very much in love with him. He seemed to have lost all sense of reality and, angry as I was, pity always encroached on it in the end and we continued. But I didn't recover from this incident, which not only cured me of believing Jess' statements, but also made me mistrusting of everyone. Once, I had known people who told the truth. Now, I was convinced that something in me provoked lies and I lost confidence in myself.

There were moments of light relief, though, such as seeing Jess' astonishment when I told him there were three Sitwells, not four. 'But Elaine,' he said, 'there's Edith, Satchel, Osbert and Sir Sheverell.'

I had to break the news that there were indeed Edith and Osbert and Sacheverell but no one called Satchel. Jess was disappointed.

'Oh, I thought one of them had been knighted.'

There were also moments that perturbed me, like the day, six weeks after our marriage, when many of Jess' friends stopped speaking to me. I only discovered ten years later, when I was separated from Jess, that he had told everyone, 'I love my wife but it makes me sad that she makes me sleep on the floor.' This piece of information was broken to me in Victoria Street, in London, when I met one of our first hotel clients, Dr Michael Winstanley, late Liberal MP for Cheadle Hulme in Cheshire.

He said, 'Hello Elaine, I was thinking about you the other day when I saw the publicity pictures in the paper. I heard that you were separated from Jess.'

I said yes I was.

'I never thought it would work,' said Dr Winstanley, 'especially after he told everyone you made him sleep on the floor.'

The shock was so great that Jess had told such a lie a month and a half into the marriage that I cried like a baby in the middle of Victoria Street. Michael Winstanley led me to a bar, gave me a coffee and said, 'I'm very sorry, I thought you knew.'

I never saw the knife in the back and I still don't.

Often, when the creditors had gone away, Jess relaxed and made us some hot chocolate. It was his new habit in the second year of our marriage. I never suspected anything, even when once, after a particularly large dose of hot chocolate I fell asleep in the middle of the lounge to the amusement of Jess' friends. Who knows what could have happened then.

I never thought much of it, but, one night after I had drunk my hot chocolate, I went to bed and Jess followed. I don't even remember getting into bed, but I remember clearly waking in the night and, while I could hear Jess snoring to my left, I could also feel a cold hand caressing my right shoulder and descending to my right breast.

Whatever sleeping pill Jess had put in the hot chocolate ceased to work the moment I realised that someone was in the room. I was sure that whoever it was had come to kidnap Paula, who was in her cot in the corner. I shouted to Jess to turn on the lamp at his side of the bed. The snoring ceased like magic and he threw the lamp through the open window where it smashed in the courtyard below. I ran to the door to turn on the central light. The bulb had been removed. Finally, I picked up my baby and began to cry. A door closed in the corridor. Whoever had been there had escaped.

Jess was so enraged he forgot everything in his disappointment.

'Get out and take Paula with you,' he screamed.

Stunned, I looked at his face, contorted by rage and knew that from that moment on nothing could ever be the same. I put Paula in her cot and pushed it to a nearby room and closed then locked the door. Shock made me tremble and I felt empty, sad and so very alone.

What did it all mean?

I didn't understand what Jess had wanted. Perversions were something I didn't know about at that time. The idea that a man might want to see his wife taken by other men would not have occurred to me. I sat on my bed, wide awake, guarding my daughter until five in the morning, when I had a bath and began the day. I didn't see Jess again for some time, neither did Sybil and Teddy. He had locked himself in his room, refusing everything except large plates of food... with HP sauce.

After breakfast, I was sitting outside with Paula in her pram when I noticed something small and black lying on the empty car park in front of the hotel. When I went to see what it was, I found a kitten that had been badly injured by a car. As a child, I had never been allowed to have an animal or even to approach a cat or dog, but I forgot everything I'd been taught, picked up the kitten and ran to the kitchen to ask the second chef what to do to help the injured animal.

'It can't live, throw it in the bin,' he said.

I rushed upstairs to my room, put Paula in her cot and dressed the kitten's wound. Then, when it was settled, I put the tiny animal in my pocket and Paula and I sat in the garden with him. We also had our meals with him and he slept by my bed in a shoe box lined with an old cashmere scarf. He recovered remarkably and set to work teaching me 'catmanship', for which I shall always be grateful. From that moment on, my loneliness was relieved by a kitten, who was a natural born entertainer and by my child, who was surely the most loved infant ever.

Ebony the kitten was joined by Snowy, a magnificent half-Abyssinian cat, who was given to me by my Aunt Connie. She guarded Paula's pram when she was inside, spitting with terrifying rage if anyone approached. When Paula wasn't in her pram, Snowy slept in it to keep it 'safe'. She was the only cat I ever had with whom I had total telepathy. Astonishing. She taught me an invaluable lesson: that between cats and certain owners, words are never necessary.

Jess became even more silent and withdrawn at this time. Normally, he talked all the time, even when there was no one there. Now he simply sat in his room, looking out at the estuary and dreaming of London. He didn't want to discuss his problems. He talked only of the happy days we had had in London. He knew, however, that Sybil was counting on his presence and, apart from marrying me, he had never let her down. I tried to stay hopeful as the situation deteriorated in every direction. More and more creditors came to try and get paid.

Sybil had a new habit that drove me wild, of taking whatever she wanted of my clothes and going home with them. As she was size 44 and I a 38 I couldn't understand it. Then I discovered that, far from having taken them, she had asked Jess to give them to her and he had done so, even though he had not bought them. I charged along the corridors of the hotel, frightening the hell out of the staff, when I heard that Jess had also given his mother the cashmere pullovers he had bought for me in a Liberty's sale. However many times I tried to explain to him that you cannot give the same present to two people, he continued to buy presents for me and then to give them to Sybil. A few years later, Jess bought me a beautiful dress that had been worn by Brigitte Bardot in a film. He took endless photos of me in this dress. Then he gave it to Paula. Many years afterwards, someone claimed he had also given it to her. To Jess, this was perfectly normal behaviour. He simply couldn't understand that, once given, an object belonged to the person who had received it. It was no longer his to dispose of as he pleased.

The truth of the situation, excluding the endless guests walking out of the hotel and endless creditors standing in the hall, was that Jess loved his mum too much to be married. He had not grasped that mother-love and married-love are different and the stress my presence provoked contributed, with all the other problems, to his vulnerability. This was not all. The terrible violence lurking under the surface, the abnormal reasoning and erratic behaviour were signs of mental illness, though at the time I tried hard to pretend that it wasn't the case.

Looking back with the wisdom of hindsight, I realise now that my problems with Sybil were mostly my own fault. We were both iron willed and forceful. Neither could yield a centimetre. If I had my time over again, I would ignore her hostility, take her out for fabulous lunches, visits to the beauty parlour and to openings of new fashion shops. The only time I ever did something frivolous with her – a trip to Liverpool for a fashion show, a deluxe lunch and a celebrity party – Sybil said it was one of the best days of her life. It was my fault for not understanding that she had dreams which had never been realised, but it takes a lifetime to learn how to handle difficult people and to know that confrontation isn't always the answer, because intelligent people learn to circumnavigate obstacles.

Jess worked on the basis of telling each person what they wanted to hear and gave each woman what he had already given to another. It was his manner of showing that someone was important. The fact that he said the same thing to ten people in a day never troubled him, neither did giving the same present to six people one after the other. The only exception to this behaviour was that he only ever married me! Many wanted to marry him and no doubt he promised them everything. In later years, it became his habit to send frantic messages for me to come and get rid of these girls! The inside of his head must have been a cauldron of boiling brain.

The days were not all black at the hotel. I still remember the arrival of the light entertainment comic, Ted Ray. He was an elegant man, dressed in tweeds and carrying his golf clubs. He had an eager-beaver look and a Bob Hope chin. On telling the receptionist that he had a week's booking, she laughed so much, she couldn't hand him his key. I hurried forward to take over and burst into peals of laughter when he spoke. Ashamed of myself, I offered to take him to his room, apologising on the way up the stairs for having laughed.

He said, 'Don't worry Mrs Yates, people always laugh, even before I speak.'

And they did. Despite my efforts at self-control, I tee-heed every time he passed, as did the staff and most of the guests. It was a memorable week. Jess often got celebrities to come to the hotel to help publicise it, one of whom was Hughie Green.

The alarm signal on Jess' deteriorating mental health came in the third year of the marriage, when we'd gone to the first floor to look at the newly decorated River Wing bedrooms. Jess was pleased with them and I was happy that he seemed content. We decided to have a pot of tea and some ginger parkin in the private lounge on the ground floor and then go to the pictures. Heading towards the main staircase with its fine wooden balustrade, I put my hand on the rail and suddenly Jess pushed me hard, making me fall all the way to the ground floor. The fall caused a haemorrhage, but no broken bones. The shock, however, was profound and it was months before I could bring myself to think of that moment. Until then, I cried. The most distressing part was that Jess remembered nothing at all of the incident when the doctor tried to question him. In case the haemorrhage had been caused by an early pregnancy, I went into hospital for a few days. I never succeeded in having another child, though I dreamed of having many. I'm very proud that Paula had four beautiful daughters, each one interesting and full of different talents. I love my grandchildren very much.

I didn't fully realise it at the time, but the staircase incident marked the beginning of the end of our marriage. Up to that point, I had not thought of separation. I was not daunted by the task of bringing up Paula on my own.

From that moment, Jess stayed mostly in his room drinking tea and watching television. He refused to see the creditors, or to sign any cheques, and told me to sign in his name, which I did, after having checked each one with Sybil. The family finally decided that the hotel must be put on the market because of the worsening financial situation and Jess' increasingly disturbed behaviour. When I told him that the hotel was to be sold Jess was happy for a few days. He photographed Paula for hours and asked to go on picnics to an old quarry he adored.

Months passed and the tension mounted because no one wanted to buy the hotel. I did my best to make light of the situation to Jess, but could see that he was more and more withdrawn from reality. In my heart, I now knew that the marriage might not survive, that it could change but would never be the same. The young girl Jess had loved, whose radiance and innocence had fascinated him, was now a woman who no longer wanted to live on the quicksand of his troubled mind. I wanted to be alone and at peace with Paula. After years spent sobbing because I didn't know how to deal with very stressful situations, I no longer cried. I made decisions and did my best to implement them and my most important decision was to buy a tiny house for Paula and me, in case Jess' condition worsened. I asked my father to help me and he put up what money he had and I found the rest when the time came. Having made my plans, I telephoned around the estate agents and asked if they could find me a tiny, inexpensive cottage with a garden in the Conway area.

After the episode of the staircase, I was afraid of Jess, because his aggressive reaction had come at a moment when he seemed calm. Sometimes, we were still happy. Jess played the piano wonderfully and often I danced for him when the end-of-season guests had all gone. He believed we could be happy again, if only we could return to London. Ever the realist, I knew we never could, because we'd changed and I had understood what my grandad had meant when he talked of never knowing a man until you've had your back to the wall in his company. I now knew that when Jess had his back to the wall, he left me to it and went home to his mother. I still loved him, but not as a wife. I loved him as I would have loved a sick child and that troubled me as did his ever increasing talk of revenge. Jess had always liked thinking about how he could do down people whom he considered had been unkind to him. It made him happy to write lists of everyone who had upset him, so he could take revenge on those who had 'crossed' him when the business was sold. Daily, he wrote letters that I had to type and sign to show his mother to prove I was in agreement with him. These letters, dictated by Jess and, much later, my own written under his instructions, when I was travelling – 'Write as if you're a criminal, or better still, Al Capone' –Jess amused himself by instructing me. They were my first works of fiction, but I didn't realise it. When I didn't write as he wanted and what he wanted me to say he was frightening to say the least. It was a side of him that sat at odds with his public image, that of a kind of benign, avuncular figure, who had started his television career with a programme for the BBC's children's department called *Junior Film Club* and then gone on to appear in such series as *The Good Old Days*, *Top Down*, *Come Dancing* and *Stars on Sunday*, of which more later. He could be just as pleasant at home, until he wanted something that he couldn't have. Then, his screaming rages were as destructive as those of a spoilt child.

Jess had once made everyone laugh. The metamorphosis into a hate-filled, rancorous character reminded me of my mother. What upset me most was that he seemed to be trapped in a state of eternal adolescence. All his lies, his defiance of and reliance on his mother or of me and his need to trick intelligent people were indications of the time warp that prevented him growing up. He never did grow up and neither did his daughter. Now I hated Jess' habit of tripping up waiters, friends and family as they passed by. It was far from funny and the problem of the purgatives and sedatives he had dosed me with ended only after the incident with the intruder in our bedroom that I woken from, when I refused to eat or drink anything he handed me. This caused a row, but I held firm. Thwarted, Jess was very difficult to live with. At the beginning of our marriage, his ignorance and lack of formal education had made me forgive him almost everything, until I realised that his insouciance was also a lie, fabricated and unreal, like the rest.

One evening, I went into the hotel kitchen at nine-thirty to get a cold meal that had been left by the chef for two guests who had warned us of their late arrival. As I put out my hand to take the plate with its silver cover, a big rat leaped out and nearly gave me a heart attack. I immediately rang Sybil and Teddy, who arranged for a Rentokil team to inspect and act immediately. The result? The whole hotel was said to be 'full of rat tunnels'. Sybil kept looking behind her, as if King Rat were waiting to eat her whole. Teddy remained impassive. After midget submarines in the war, a rat or two, or 200, didn't bother him.

We didn't tell Jess at first, because due to the stress caused by the difficulty of selling the hotel, he had suffered a return of 'stink'. After a couple of weeks of rat extermination, the two front lounges were invaded by a stink of their own, as if Jess' were not enough. Urgent investigation by the exterminators showed that poisoned rats had infiltrated the space beneath the floorboards and were rotting away. Teams of men came at night to remove the dead rats and to try to make the hotel habitable.

Anxious to get out of the place, one windy afternoon, I went with Paula and a local estate agent to the Roewen Valley to look at a cheap cottage that was for sale. It had one big room, no upstairs and a very pretty garden. When I saw how tiny it was, I felt claustrophobic and said I didn't think it would do. The agent, a man with a lot of business

Top left: Nana with my mother in 1917.

Top right: Gertrude and me in 1937.

Bottom left: My first theatre appearance (I'm second from the left in the front row).

Bottom right: With baby Paula.

Top left: In the Bardot dress Jess gave me and four other ladies.

Top right: A photo from the mid 60s.

Bottom left: The author photo by John D Green used on some of my book covers.

Bottom right: At a Bluebell rehearsal in 1956, trying to keep balance on the high heels.

Top left: A publicity shot for Yorkshire TV.

Top right: Dancing at a cabaret in Jersey.

Bottom: On location in Yugoslavia. © *Rex*

Paula and Bob in 1980.
©*Rex*

Top left: Paula on holiday in Marbella where she learned to swim.

Top right: Paula and me in the grounds of her English school in Majorca.

Bottom: Jess and I with our mothers at our wedding.

Top: With a beautiful photo of the girl with the blue glass eyes.

Bottom: Hughie, Paula, Jess and me.

Top: Happy times as a young Family.

Right: With the painting I did for Paula that she never got to see.

Vive la France! I adore the peace of La Cadière d'Azur, a world away from the noise and traffic fumes of London.

experience, smiled as if he'd known in advance how I would react. Then he put me and Paula back in his Bentley and began to negotiate the narrow lanes back to Conway.

A hundred yards from the cottage I saw a 'For Sale' notice and behind it banks of the most beautiful rhododendrons flanking a long, narrow drive. When I asked to see the house, the agent told me that he didn't have the key, but that he would be selling it by auction in forty-eight hours' time. We drove up the drive so that I could look at the house from the outside and I fell in love with the garden, the isolated position in a niche on the hillside. Above all else, I loved the silence and the peace. I had been dreaming for so long about peace and security and, as I stood there, gazing up at the house, I thought I'd found them. The only sounds were birds twittering and the baaing of sheep on the hillside opposite. I tried to tell myself that I'd been happy in the past and could be happy again in the future, if I made an effort, got out of the hotel and into a new phase of my life.

On my return to the hotel, I telephoned my mother-in-law and asked to see her. I didn't know how much Sybil knew about the deterioration in the marriage, so I told her the truth, that I wanted a house for Paula and me, with or without Jess, that I could raise a certain sum and wanted to bid in the auction in less than two days' time. I said the marriage was not a success and had been running downhill for a while, that the main problem was Jess' mental instability and the fact that I had grown up and changed irrevocably. I said I was willing to do whatever would keep Paula happy, but in the case of a divorce, I wanted custody of the child. I left Sybil's house uncertain as to whether she would help me or not. I knew I would need her support to get Jess to let me buy the house.

As I had never seen inside the house, I was unaware that a burst water pipe had left a trail of green fungus along one wall and that people who had gone to view the place had thought this indicative of wet rot. Many had lost interest immediately. At the auction, I asked Jess to bid for me and told him my limit. There was only one opposing bidder, but my limit was soon reached. I was astonished to see Jess continuing to bid at a signal from his mother. Sybil put in the same sum as I did and we signed together for the property, the deeds being in our joint names. As Sybil didn't like fuss and emotion, I did my best not to show how astounded and touched I was by her action and simply thanked her. Then, driving Jess back to the hotel, my joy and elation were tempered with caution. How would we get on living in the former country house of the Bibby shipping family, a house that could very easily be divided in two. Could Sybil and I find a base to live amicably? I was prepared to try if she was. Then, I asked myself if Jess would move in, too, or would he want to return to work in London when the hotel was sold. And would I go with him? But I no longer wanted to live with my husband. Something had died in the relationship during the five years at the hotel. I still admired Jess' formidable talents as a musician, photographer, producer and raconteur of genius, but he had run off every time there was trouble and I'd learned to get by alone.

The hotel receptionist was Irish, full of charm and with a vivid imagination. One day, she asked me if she could come catch a lift in to the neighbouring town because she wanted to see a clairvoyant. I said of course she could come, surprised, even so, that such an intelligent and seemingly conventional young woman should want to see such a person. I can't think of anything worse than being told the future. I like thinking about it, at least I did when I was young, because I was sure it couldn't be worse than the present or the past.

I stopped the car in front of the clairvoyant's house and Catherine went in. Fifteen minutes later she reappeared, her eyes wide with wonder. 'She's a magic person, madam. You're to go in now. I've paid for you to see her as you were kind enough to drive me here.'

Every form of foreboding hit me and I was tempted to drive away fast. Then I decided well, why not. Catherine had told me the lady was Russian and that, above all, touched my curiosity.

She was old and wrinkled, with a face that had suffered and survived, a beautiful face, lit by a rare, inner luminosity. When I entered she shook hands, gave a violent start and then led me to the living room and after looking again briefly at the hand she had shaken, she focused on my face. There were no crystal balls or other horseshit, just a woman with a fascinating accent, who had created a typically Russian home in the middle of Wales. Her voice was low and she rolled her rrrrs like Edith Piaf.

'I have never seen such a horrible childhood. If you survived that you'll survive everything! But your life is going to change radically. A few months from now, you'll be thousands of miles away from here. And soon you'll live in a big house surrounded by many tall trees, where you will be very lonely. You will take up a profession to counteract the loneliness and it's a good idea because it will enable you to be independent for many years. Then, far, far in the future, you will change profession. At that time also you will meet a man who will influence all the rest of your life. He is very pernickety. He arranges things on his desk, or by his bed, as if he has measured every little space. He is difficult and you are not easy either, but you will understand each other and you will work at your new profession with his support. But all that is very far in the future.'

Indeed it was, because the man she described was Monsieur, my French second husband whom I met over twenty years later.

'In the meantime,' she went on, 'take care, because there is a man who wants to keep you for ever and he will be dangerous.'

I mulled over all these strange prophecies, as she poured tea from an old samovar. She was a fascinating and sympathetic woman, who seemed to read the thoughts in my head. When the time came to leave, she said, 'Try not to worry too much. You have some very difficult times ahead, but you'll go through them all like a warrior woman. You will change everything around you and then you'll change yourself and become the person you were destined to be, not the one you are now. At this moment you are the woman he wants you to be.'

It seems ironic that many years later, when Paula was co-hosting *The Big Breakfast*, she, too, should have discovered a psychic whose comments she found equally accurate. I had told her that, although this Russian lady's words had been prophetic for me, I still remained sceptical of psychics in general and advised her to keep her distance from them because for the most part they were con artists.

I drove back to the hotel in silence, conscious that the Russian psychic had, by whatever magic means, hit the nail on the head of what really troubled me in the marriage. Jess wanted a tightly corseted, platform-brassiered, walking sexual invitation for a wife. He saw himself as a Hollywood character, such as the scriptwriter and studio mogul Daryl Zanuck, or better still, Al Capone as portrayed by Damon Runyan, one of his favourite writers. He lived in a Walter Mitty world where he was a tough cookie surrounded by Mafia henchmen and luscious, libidinous chicks who would erotically perform in his studio. Once, to tease him for his admiration of Al Capone, Dutch Schultz and company, I got two actor friends and rigged them out in classic Mafia outfits and then borrowed a friend's big black car. I asked the actors to sit in the car all morning near the entrance to the house, sure that Jess would laugh like a gong at the joke. Instead, he panicked, told everyone I had got a Mafia hit squad to kill him and locked himself in his room for days, unable to eat because of blind terror. Jess, who had always loved way-out jokes, could no longer recognise one, even when I explained what I had done. He had told so many tall tales to so many people that he now told one more, seeing himself as the Fugitive and asking everyone to protect him.

I asked Jess repeatedly to see a psychiatrist, as did our family doctor. The situation was almost the exact duplicate of my mother's, because each time anyone asked him to take advice from a psychiatrist Jess became violent. On this occasion, he hit me with a decorator's plank across the knees when I was carrying the tea tray back to the kitchen. The doctor came, but Jess had gone to his mother's. Fortunately, Paula never saw any of these incidents. For all Jess' lack of control, he was still cunning enough to avoid attacking me when there were witnesses around. Paula had her own little world in which to play, with our cats and the friends she made among the staff, who included a couple of very petite chambermaids who came from Trento in Italy. Paula liked being with them so much she pretended that she was a chambermaid, too. It wasn't until she went to school that she actually found some friends who were her own age.

After the incident with the plank, I couldn't walk for the

grotesquely swollen knees and stayed in bed for days trying to work out how to protect myself when I couldn't even run away.

Shortly afterwards, I received an urgent message from my Aunt Marjorie to come at once to see my grandad George, who was very ill in hospital. The previous year, Nana had died in her sleep. George, having woken, as always, at quarter to five, had a bit of difficulty dislodging Nana's hand from his chest. When he turned on the light, he realised that she had died where she had always slept, in his arms.

From that moment on, George saw no reason to live.

'The light has gone from my life Elaine,' he told me. 'I shall do my best to rejoin Constance as quickly as possible.'

And with his iron will and his passionate desire for death, he managed to become ill, then very ill and now terminally ill.

I called a man friend, who lived near to our house, Plas Yn Roe, and who had a helicopter and explained the situation. He sent the helicopter and his pilot and we took off and, an hour later, landed on the hospital lawn. I ran towards a big window, where I could see George, in his best dressing gown, standing to attention in his usual military style. I nearly burst into tears and had to impose George's precious discipline on myself. I gave him a big kiss and he sat on the edge of the bed and said, earnestly, 'Elaine, I asked you to come because they think I've gone mad. They can't see those boats at the far end of the room, a lot of boats, a regatta perhaps and the sea looks rough.'

I looked down the long room and said, 'You're right; it's a regatta and a very big one.'

Sighing with relief, George fell back on his bed, exhausted. 'I knew you'd tell me the truth,' he said. And I wondered if lies were permitted to ease the agony of the dying.

We talked for a while, remembering happy days with Nana and our trips to the Trough of Bowland to walk in the hills when I was a child. Then I kissed him and let him sleep. George died the following morning. I miss him still.

A few days later, the sale of the hotel was signed and a date given for our moving out. I was jubilant. Jess returned from his mother's singing like Vera Lynn. But I felt optimistic because I wanted to have some hope in my life, not just for me but for Paula, too. Until that point, Paula had known no other home and I knew she had found it difficult, sharing me with the guests. When she wanted me to herself, she would say, 'Mummy, I want your undivided attention. Let's leave Daddy and the guests and go somewhere secret.' Even though she came with me to the office and the kitchens and we spent afternoons in the garden, where she had a paddling pool, or went to the beach, giving her my absolutely undivided attention was sometimes difficult. Just like my mother, Paula had no wish to share me with anyone.

When, at last, we all drove off down the drive of the hotel for the last time, my thoughts were focused on Jess: I wondered if he would become the real Jess again? I hoped very much for a miracle.

CHAPTER TWELVE

A few months after leaving the hotel, Jess got a brief work contract to do some television coverage on the making of a US–Yugoslav co-production. I was taken on as a bit-part player so that I could accompany him. On our arrival, one of the technicians, seeing my 5-inch heels and black leather coat, followed me around begging to be whipped. The wife of a leading light on the film asked for me to be sent back to England immediately as her husband was obsessed. I'd never been alone, or even in conversation with the man, but she kept on insisting. Jess took hundreds of pictures of me in a costume that he had borrowed because he loved tiger skins. These photographs, from Jess' personal and private collection, often appear in the papers and I always wonder who sold them. Jess also photographed me in a field with a fjord in the distance. I hadn't realised that there was a white stallion behind me, who, when he sniffed my perfume, got an erection of Olympian proportions and clunked around the field wondering where to put it.

In the adjacent field, many of the unit horses were grazing and my perfume affected all of them, too. Jess became so excited by the sight of such animal lust that he, too, got an erection that knocked over the tripod, letting his precious Rolleiflex camera fall to the ground. Anguish at the possibility of damaging the camera put paid to Jess' erection, but the horses continued running around with their willies wobbling in the wind like dozens of king cobras. Watching Yugoslav stuntmen laughed in hysterics at Jess, the horses and me. The photographs never appeared. Perhaps Jess forgot to put a second reel in his camera!

I only remembered this incident recently when, walking down the hill of La Cadière d'Azur, I saw two chestnut stallions in a field. They came to the gate bordering the road to be stroked and given a biscuit. When my perfume hit them, their willies appeared in all their splendour and waved in the wind as the others had in Yugoslavia thirty years previously. Unfortunately for me, there were some Swiss tourists at the gate and all of them turned to see who had provoked this equine reaction. Embarrassed, I rushed all the way back home to avoid the necessity for explanations!

The biggest laugh came when the American company built some lavatories for the unit in the woods so that the extras would have somewhere to go for privacy. The loos made a terrible noise when they flushed and were shunned completely by the Yugoslavs, who continued to go *pi-pi* and *ca-ca* on the hillside, in full view of everyone. This stunned the American members of the unit, who had not bargained for such a primitive lack of inhibition. The unit manager sent out orders that they use the new toilets but to no avail. Champion level farts and cheers of pleasure for a job well done continued to entertain us lesser mortals.

The end of this venture came in Belgrade when two unit chauffeurs failed to arrived to take me to the set and I took coffee with an American actor whom I had never met before. Later, I was called to the unit office, admonished and shortly thereafter put on a plane for England. I didn't mind. I had no vocation for acting. I can't act. I can dance and do one or two other things well, but working in front of dozens of technicians, adorable though they all were, was my idea of hell.

I dreamed more and more of working alone, of being invisible as I had when small. Still, I wanted desperately to learn to earn my living, so I could leave Jess and live with Paula. But how? What could I do that would be stable? Later, I did take a couple of film parts in Italy and had one interesting experience over there. It was enriching, because after a meeting with the film director Visconti and taking advice from him, suddenly I knew what I wanted to do in the future, but not how to do it. I wanted to write, but would I be able to?

Of Yugoslavia, two people have remained in my mind over the years: the first was a young actress called Talitha Pol (later Talitha Getty), who was fabulously beautiful with great charisma , but who was also given to bouts of sadness and often cried like a child. Once, I tried to comfort her, but it was obvious that Talitha was searching for something she would never find. The other person who impressed me was Professor Bluma T. Trell, a former professor of ancient Greek and Roman History at the University of New York and an expert on numismatics, the study of coins and notes. Bluma was on the set with her husband, Max, a writer, and we became great friends, seeing each other on and off over the years. Later, when I separated from Jess, it was Bluma Trell who said, 'You're beautiful, but beauty doesn't last. You're lucky to have a brain and a sense of humour, use them! Go write your book and show it to me when it's done.'

She was seventy-four when I met her, as was her husband. I was in my late twenties. On age, Bluma said, 'I don't notice my age. I just ignore it. The only difference between how I am now and how I was at thirty is that I tire much faster.'

How true. Now I'm older, I feel exactly the same, or better than I did when I was thirty, but I tire 'much faster', as she said. Very much faster! Bluma was a remarkable woman, married to a very wise man.

I am the world's worst singer. I have always been a terrible singer and I always will be. A member of my family once said to me, 'Elaine, if you're going to sing, go into the garden, or you'll start the dog barking.' I dream of singing like Edith Piaf, or Charles Aznavour, or anyone at all, except me. Imagine my terror when, later that year – it was 1966 – after the trip to Yugoslavia, Jess announced that he was going to teach me to sing, get me a recording contract and be my accompanist.

'I won't do it, you know I can't sing.'

'Of course you can,' he replied. 'Anyway, with a chest measurement like yours who needs to sing?'

For weeks, Jess rehearsed me, insisting that I sing French songs with a French accent. I could keep the melody, but the starting note had to be hammered out hard, or I started an octave lower. He chose dresses from Berman's, the film costumiers, who loaned me Ursula Andress' clothes, or Anita Ekberg's, as my heavyweight boxer's shoulders wouldn't fit anyone else's. Then, when he considered that I was ready, Jess arranged for me to be tried out at the Leeds City Varieties.

I was so traumatised by the idea of having to sing in public that all I did well was my entrance and my final bow. I don't remember the rest, except that about two bars from the end of the final number I saw that Jess was standing up to play the piano and wondered what the dickens he was doing. Veins stood out on his forehead and he was sweating profusely. It was then that

I realised that the piano was moving inexorably forwards on the gradient of the stage and that Jess was hanging on to it and wedging it with his right leg, while continuing to play for me with true professionalism. I sang faster and faster, praying not to be hit by the piano in case its movement accelerated. Then I took my bow, profoundly relieved when the curtains closed and two stagehands ran on, secured the piano and gave Jess a chair. From there, he proceeded to send everyone into convulsions of laughter by explaining his predicament. Only Jess with his inimitable sense of humour could have got away with it: 'I held the piano as best I was able with my right leg, but my right ball got trapped. And the more the piano moved the more it squeezed my ball. It'll be swollen like a melon in the morning. It will probably be black and blue.'

It was. Jess decided to put some embrocation on his right ball and sent himself through the roof with a burning sensation that lasted all night. We certainly had reason to remember my debut!

I was then asked to perform in a London supper club. I hated the cigarette smoke, and being so close to the audience, but above all having to sing. I had nightmares every night and dreaded each new day. I told Jess that I no longer wanted to sing, ever.

'There's a man to see you,' he replied. 'He's very well known as a recording manager and he wants to offer you a three-year contract.'

I've tried very hard to remember this man's name, but apart from his first name, David, I can't bring it to mind. He was respected in the business for his vast experience and his gift for talent spotting. When I turned down the three-year contract, he was angry, but I couldn't bear to think that my future might be singing into a microphone and going in front of live audiences. I should have taken it, I suppose. I might have made a fortune with my frog-with-piles voice. But I'm made for silence and solitude, not the endless recording, touring and performing life that pays so well but costs so much in physical wear and tear. Obviously, I was on the back row when God handed out the talent for making money. I was made to be a hermit, not a sequined singer. At least marriage taught me that.

It was about now that I was asked to go see the film director, Federico Fellini, in Rome. He had seen a publicity photo in a magazine and wished to interview me. I had always thought of Fellini as a big, fat man with a lion's head and abundant talent. I did not know that he, like Jess, was a pathological liar. Jess lied to prove his supremacy over intellectuals, by making them believe everything he said, no matter how improbable or impossible. Fellini lied like a child, describing what he wanted to happen but not what was going to. His erotic fantasies were just that, fantasies. I don't think he ever wanted them to come true or sought to delve too far into their origins. What was important was that he had asked to see me and I felt honoured. I was unaware at the time that Fellini's favourite occupation was interviewing every actor, actress, dwarf, transvestite, alcoholic, tourist and mafioso, real or imagined, in Europe.

With Paula with Jess back home, I booked into the Hilton, expecting to be in the city for about forty-eight hours, but there was no call from Fellini. I moved into a cheaper hotel in the city and a week passed, but there was still no news from Fellini. I had checked up on his way of working and had been told by everyone that he was disorganised, full of ideas for films he would never make and that he liked preparing films but not starting them. In fact, what I'd learned about Fellini made him sound more and more like Jess.

I couldn't afford to stay on indefinitely waiting for his call, so I decided to go to the studio where he was doing some work, the Safa Palatino in the centre of Rome. Fellini wouldn't take calls, or make appointments at that time, but I went anyway and hailing a handsome man who was passing said, 'I have an interview with Fellini at six- thirty, will you take me to his office?'

Once inside a very ordinary office, the slim, dark man said, 'I'm Fellini, now who are you?'

I stared at the slim body, the very handsome face and said without thinking, 'I thought you were big and fat.'

He replied without the slightest hesitation, 'Usually I am big and fat, but I did a diet and now I am thin. Tell me who you are?'

We talked, and he remembered asking one of his assistants if they could arrange for him to see me as a result of my visit to the Cannes Film Festival in May. He showed me a pile of photos from the 6,000 applicants from all over the world.

'You can send in a photograph,' he said.

'No,' I replied, increasingly annoyed with this elusive mountain. 'I'm not rich. I can't stay in Rome for months waiting for you to decide to start if you aren't going to use me, so decide.'

He stared at me, as if seeing me for the first time. 'What a terrible woman; the other British persons I've met were very polite.'

'You don't need a photo to decide.'

'Well, you come to my hotel at eight-thirty this evening and pretend you are something interesting. Make your own dialogue and I'll follow your lead. That is your test.'

I asked him if he were trying to seduce me. He said no, he didn't need to go to an hotel to do that. What he wanted was to be surprised.

I returned to the hotel, wondering what to make of such a weird request. Fellini didn't need subterfuge to seduce women, when half of Europe was dreaming of a part, however minute, in his film. Fellini functioned on a level unknown to ordinary people. It wasn't that he was particularly interested in sex – he had a very odd relationship with his wife, Giulietta, who was an actress and who tended to dominate him – and I suspected that what he really wanted more than anything was, indeed, to be astounded. I decided to do my best to make myself unforgettable.

First, I borrowed a dress from an American friend, called Nan, whom I had met at Babington's Tea Rooms in the Piazza di Spagna. She came from somewhere down in the southern states and was well known for her astonishing wardrobe. We added yards of cloud grey and black tulle that we fitted around my head and shoulders so only my eyes were visible. The dress was black, loose fitting and diaphanous. I went by taxi to the hotel, though it wasn't very far from where I was staying. When I asked for Maestro Fellini, I was shown up with great pomp.

Fellini opened the door, gave a big smile and then, peering into the clouds of tulle, said, 'Is it you Elena?'

'I am the Angel of Death,' I replied, as I walked in, closed the door, locked it and pocketed the key.

Fellini looked decidedly uncomfortable. 'Are you going to take off your clothes, or shall I cut them off you?' I asked. I felt very empowered. Life with Jess and some part-time work with the firm Theo Cowan Public Relations, where I worked with a number of stars, had taught me how to handle famous egos.

Fellini ran to the door to escape, forgetting that the key was in my pocket. He said, 'Look, I give you the role. We start tomorrow.'

I turned out the lights and drew all the curtains but the

one on a small side window. Fellini ran for the bathroom, but I got there first. He screamed for help, loud enough to wake the phantoms in his imaginary past. No one came. Fellini's reputation for strange behaviour was such that I could have cut his throat ten times over and walked out and no one would have suspected anything. Instead, when he was in mid-scream, I rammed a candlestick from the sideboard in his back and said, 'And now I'm going to kill you.' The screams rose up in a shattering crescendo. Then the 'Maestro' fell to his knees and begged me to spare his life.

At that moment, I took off the veiled head-dress that was nearly suffocating me, turned on the lights, opened the curtains and said, 'Well, what are we going to eat for dinner?'

Fellini stared at me, stunned his face ashen as he dropped into an armchair. For a while he looked hard at me and then he said, 'Why did you do that?'

'You said I should write my own dialogue,' I replied. 'Perhaps you expected me to seduce you. Anyone can do that, it's natural and doesn't need acting ability. I decided to surprise you.'

He rose up, roaring with annoyance, 'You nearly terrify me to a heart attack!'

'I'm glad I acted well enough to do it.'

Fellini couldn't eat his dinner, but as time passed, he saw the funny side of what had happened and said, as I was leaving, 'I give you two or three days' work with another

English monster. You will get on well. We don't start Monday, but in four weeks' time, so come to the studio tomorrow and I give you her phone number and a letter for the costumier.'

'I'm not rich and it's hard for me to stay here, so start on time or else.'

Fellini smiled wanly and whispered, 'No one ever play such a trick on me. No one. You frighten me so much I shall have nightmares. Giulietta will notice and ask questions.'

I left the hotel, satisfied that at least Fellini wouldn't forget me.

The next day, I met the English actress, who was married to an Italian lawyer. Tiny, blonde and bewitching, she had a collection of ancient and modern pornography that was the envy of many collectors. Jess would certainly have died with envy. Later, we worked together briefly on the Fellini set, in my case very briefly. I was happy to have made it, but the experience turned me off the cinema for ever. I don't know if I'm in the film, or on the cutting-room floor. What mattered to me was that I had been chosen. I was one of the ones who had passed muster out of those 6,000 who had only dreamed. After the demolition of my confidence during my marriage to Jess, symbolically, it meant a great deal to me.

When I had finished my work, I went to say goodbye to Fellini, who kissed me with affection and said, 'Elena, you want to come to the hotel tonight? I would so like to be surprised. What will you think of next? Perhaps you make me laugh, you're good at that.'

It was a joke, of course. You can only pull a stunt like that once in a lifetime.

CHAPTER THIRTEEN

One night, while I was in Rome waiting for filming to start, I dined with a South American woman friend, at a hotel in the centre of the city. As we came out of the hotel and were walking to the waiting taxi, I was pushed aside by a man in an elegant tuxedo. He was in his sixties, with white hair and watchful, hawk-like eyes. He wanted the taxi and that was all that mattered to him. Rather the worse for wear, he slammed the door in my face and was driven away. As he disappeared from view, I saw that he had dropped his wallet. Picking it up, I put it in my shoulder bag and waited with Dina for the next taxi to appear.

Walking from her apartment back to my place, which was only 50 yards away, I was still annoyed by the man's ruthless manner that had seemed at odds with his studied, gentlemanly appearance. Once inside my apartment, having survived the 109 steps from the street, I took a shower and selected a book to read in bed. Then I opened the wallet. There were two letters addressed to the man, some money, bankers' orders and diverse other indications of his wealth. His was a household name in Britain, though his face was less known. He was Charles Clore, the financier. I telephoned the society columnist of the local English language newspaper and asked if he knew where the man was staying. He gave me the name and address of the hotel, which was less than 100 yards from my apartment and I decided to go there in the morning.

After an hour or two's enjoyment with Lawrence Durrell's *Bitter Lemons of Cyprus*, I turned out the light, but couldn't sleep. It was very hot and humid and I kept thinking, 'What if a burglar arrives and steals all the bankers' drafts and money.' Finally, I got up an hour earlier than usual, at four, made coffee and took my morning shower.

At nine-thirty, I went to the hotel and asked to see Mr Clore (he was not yet knighted). I was led upstairs and found him in a silk dressing gown and pyjamas, eating breakfast. He glanced at me and spoke in a rough way with a curious accent that I later told him was 'elocutioned' East End.

'What do you want?'

'Your wallet fell out of your pocket last night when you were getting into the taxi.'

'I was in a hurry. Why didn't you give it to the head porter?'

'Every morning when I go to the paper shop to buy the *Daily American* and the stamps for my daily letter to my daughter, they short-change me. I think it's a habit in the city, a way of making insupportably arrogant tourists acceptable. So I wouldn't have trusted anyone to give you the wallet.'

'How much do you want?'

'You're an ill-mannered, uncouth yobbo and no great credit to your famous name.'

Charles Clore paused mid-mouthful and looked hard at me, as if he wasn't sure that he had heard right. Then he opened the wallet, extracted the cash and threw it over the table at me. It fell on the floor. I could have done with the money to pay for my unexpectedly extended stay, but his way of throwing it at me defeated my practicality and I got up and made for the door, leaving the notes lying here and there where he had thrown them. Charles called after me.

'Where are you going?'

'Home.'

'Come here.'

His voice was harsh and he looked red and angry. I paused at the door of the suite, looked back at him and then hurried out. Charles rushed after me and shouted down the corridor.

'Why are you leaving like that?'

'Because it's Sunday and Sunday isn't my day for meeting horrible, ill-mannered old bastards.'

I rushed out of the hotel and went to the English Church in the Via del Babuino to say a prayer for Paula and another for me, in order not to have a heart attack brought on by my annoyance at the Englishman. Then I went home and found friends waiting to take me swimming at Fregene, the seaside resort half an hour from the centre of Rome. In a few seconds I'd forgotten the horrible, ill-mannered, old bastard. I was unaware that he had sent his man to see where I lived.

A few days later, I received a large box containing an exquisite Ungaro evening dress. No note. A few days later, another large box and another dress. This time there was a note that read, 'The horrible, ill-mannered, old bastard presents his excuses. I'm leaving Rome, but I'll be back.'

A month or so later, just before my departure from Italy, I went to lunch by the pool at the Hilton Hotel with a group of American friends, whom I had met on the Via Veneto when having a coffee. It was the norm then for English and American visitors to strike up friendly conversations which often ended with groups of people getting together later on to socialise. That day the group included the Hollywood mogul Daryl Zanuck, whom I adored because his cigar was bigger than he was and because he was so precise in his arrangements. Each time he took me to lunch, he rang once: 'This is Mr Zanuck. I shall be leaving my hotel in ten minutes.' Then a second call: 'This is Mr Zanuck. I shall be leaving the hotel in five minutes.' Then, sometimes, 'This is Mr Zanuck, I shall be three minutes later than scheduled. I shall be outside your apartment in my usual car at 1.03 precisely.' Ah, that's how I like them!

After lunch, the Zanuck party lay back to rest in the sun. I was half asleep when an Italian strolled over and dropped a water beetle on my stomach. As some members of the party were asleep in their bathing costumes, I kept quiet, brushing off the beetle as if I'd barely noticed it. Five minutes later, the Italian returned with three water beetles and dropped one on my stomach, one on my neck and one on my face. I remember getting up fast and landing him a great resounding wallop on the chin. His eyes rolled upwards and he fell in a faint, hitting the back of his head on the concrete of the pool. Zanuck bit on his cigar and said softly, 'Jesus Christ!' Then, for what seemed to me like three weeks, but was really only a matter of minutes, the maître d' of the pool's restaurant ran in and out with the latest news. 'He ees steel unconscious, signora.' Then, finally, 'He wake, signora, and he run away.'

On returning home, I found a uniformed chauffeur sitting in a large black car outside the apartment. Charles Clore was back and would be honoured if I would accompany him to dinner at the home of some friends in Monaco the following week. I would be delivered by car and returned by car to Rome the following day. I turned down the invitation because I thought I would be working the following week, though the increasing heat and humidity in Rome made me dream of going away for a few days. The chauffeur smiled when I handed him a polite note declining the invitation.

'You didn't see him, but Sir was at the Hilton for lunch today. He says you have a right hook like Tommy Farr. The Italian was unconscious for so long, Sir called his lawyers to stand by in case you needed them. Good evening, madam.'

I had no call to come to the studio the following week and due to the weather conditions and the drought, the water supply in the streets of the centre of Rome was cut to a dribble for hours each day. I half regretted not having accepted the Englishman's invitation. I had underestimated his persistence. That morning his chauffeur arrived with the request that, as I was not needed at the studios, would I like to change my mind and accompany Charles Clore to Monaco? I did.

The journey went surprisingly well. We talked about everything from his past deals to my desire to write books. The accommodation in Monaco was fabulous and the dinner at David Niven's house at Cap Ferrat spectacular. I am not a sociable person and can count on the fingers of one hand the number of times I've accepted invitations to jet-set parties, but this was an interesting group. David Niven was good looking and charming, but we didn't really talk to each other. Estée Lauder was there in a necklace of fabulous rubies and the beautiful actrees Merle Oberon appeared, looking, despite her age, as young and exquisite as ever and wearing emeralds as big as the Ritz. The men were sun-tanned, rich and for the most part predictable.

In those days, unspoken rules existed in the international set that sent them to the right place at the right time: Deauville in September, London or New York in October, Long Island in summer, the Bahamas or the Caribbean in winter for those not wanting to fall on their arses in Megève, Saint Moritz or Gstaad at Christmas. They needed each other to exist and wives and girlfriends, who did not, of course, work, talked all the time about shopping and could spend money faster than most of their owners had made it. Some of the women studied property brochures, others jewellery-auction prospectuses. All were polite, but few had a sense of humour about themselves and all of them were wearing out their teeth fast due to gnashing them at their husbands' infidelities.

Charles went to bed at midnight, exhausted by the journey and the enormous effort to be polite, well-mannered and as perfect as possible all evening. I sat on my bed, wishing I was back home at Plas Yn Roe. I had only two days' work left to do in the studios. Then I could leave Italy. In bed, I wrote a letter to Paula and wrapped up a present that I had bought her in Monaco. I woke early the following morning to see a blinding South-of-France sunrise over a China-blue sea. When he had eaten breakfast, Charles sent me to the hotel hairdresser and told me to go shopping.

'I don't need anything,' I replied.

He rolled his eyes, as though I were talking the purest nonsense.

In the salon, I was shampooed and curled and pampered, until an exotic European film star with a world-wide reputation and an ego to match told me to go away because I was sitting in her chair. I was sitting where I'd been put, so I didn't move. She shouted louder and louder as the salon director tried unsuccessfully to calm her. My silence riled her terribly and she lunged at me, but I stayed put, not wishing to use my Tommy Farr right hook or to make her kind of scene. Finally, she flounced out, happy to have been noticed by just about everyone there. Turning to make sure that she had gone, I saw the Englishman's chauffeur watching from outside the door, a huge grin on his face.

On the way back to Rome, Charles regaled me with stories of his young days and his fight to be someone. He was changed from the first time we had met, a tender, paternal attitude having appeared without my realising it. For a moment, I liked him very much and was touched by all he said. Then, when we arrived, Charles dropped me at my apartment, continued to his hotel and went from there to England. I left Rome a few days later.

Before my departure from Rome, I ate dinner with a group that included April Ashley, exquisite as always in an elegant black lace dress. April and I got on well, because she came from Liverpool and I from Blackpool and as such, we had similar mentalities and we had also both danced in Paris.

We had decided to eat a light summer dinner and were watching the passing scene, when a sailor tried to pick April up. Rising slowly, she drew herself to her full 6 feet 2 inches and bellowed, in a voice worthy of Sergeant Major Britain in his prime, 'I used to be in the fucking Marines, so watch it.' The sailor ran off, wondering where the man's voice had come from and if it were possible that under the delicate lace skirt there was something other than the tunnel of love about which he'd been dreaming.

My memories of Rome are of eating chocolate ice cream in the majestic Piazza Navona, of Sundays with friends on the beach. I remember a dinner in the garden of the American sculptress, Beverly Pepper, where I sat opposite Antonioni and next to Richard Burton, the most insecure man I ever knew. He was teaching me a poem in Welsh, when a famous Italian actress sitting opposite me stuck her foot up my dress and tried a little pedo-masturbation. And all the while Burton was reciting (I write it phonetically, because I can't spell in Welsh) 'Nant a munith gloyou loyou, on a droycli ty ar pant.' It was a surreal moment in the city that had spawned *la dolce vita*.

But Rome wasn't just about glamorous parties and handsome suitors. My worst memory of that time is undoubtedly of being raped by a famous local character, who happened to live in the street that ran parallel to mine and whose apartment backed on to the one I was staying in, which gave him every opportunity to look across at us.

He used his climbing equipment to reach the top-floor

window of my apartment. Out cold due to taking painkillers after a dental operation, I only realised what was happening towards the end of the proceedings. I was lucky. He didn't maim or mutilate me. He just entered where he wasn't welcome. I was all right for a few days. Then I left the place and moved in with friends, until I left Rome, afraid, once night came should the same thing happening again.

My last memory of the city is of being invited by a friend to go on holiday with them to Ischia. I said, 'No, I have to get back to my child, now I've worked with Fellini. I shall never do another film. I shall never leave the house again.' They laughed, because it seemed a strange thing for me to say, but it was true. Even now, I live in my home and rarely make the effort for the social life that so easily bores me.

My most mysterious souvenir of Rome, though, is of a man I never met. I was eating breakfast in the Caffé Greco, that Roman institution on a corner of the Piazza di Spagna, which was once a favourite with Keats and Shelley, when I became conscious of the intense gaze of a strangely ascetic gentleman at the other side of the room. I was young and attractive and men were curious, but the hypnotic quality of his gaze made me curious, too. He looked as if he'd seen a ghost. When I left the café, I took a good look at him and I remember thinking that he was probably an aristocrat, with his fine-boned, neurotic face and abnormally intense eyes. I next saw the man on the front page of the newspapers. He was the Marquis Casati, the brother of a

Papal Nuncio and husband of a very beautiful lady. He had killed his wife and her lover before killing himself. Everyone thought at first that it was through jealousy at being abandoned for a younger man. Then the Italian police found photos and films taken by the marquis of his wife making love with half the world, so he could take pleasure watching, filming, being the ultimate voyeur. Fascinated by the story, once I was back in Wales and interested in learning more of this kind of behavious, I went to see a consultant psychiatrist, who explained the mechanisms of a man who wants to watch his wife with other men, lots of other men. I wrote a novel on this theme called *Strange Games*, which was based on the Casati case. It was bought by a major US publisher, but proved much too strange for the conservative American readership and didn't sell well. The only light relief came when a US columnist said to me, 'Well dear, I'm glad you survived your shit of a husband.' I replied that I wasn't the Marquesa Casati, I had just used parts of the tragedy as a basis for the novel. She winked and said, 'Don't worry, dear, I shan't say a word.' But the next day, a book review printed a critic's account of the novel with photos of me and the marquesa. And suddenly I realised why the marquis had looked at me with such intensity. I could have been the sister of the wife he had, perhaps already, decided to kill.

CHAPTER FOURTEEN

Soon I was on the Emerald Isle Express on the way home. I could hardly wait to see Paula, whom I had phoned as often as I could and when I knew that she would be with her Uncle Teddy. I tried to read to pass the time I couldn't concentrate at all. When I finally saw her, she looked beautiful. She'd grown and she seemed very self-possessed. We returned to our old routines at once and went off in the car to do some food shopping. I bought a couple of Welsh quilts guaranteed for a hundred years. I still have some cushion covers of the same woven material and it's true, they seem destined to last for ever.

Paula told me that Jess and his mother had tried to make her eat during my absence and that she'd hidden food in the drawers of her bedroom. We went and cleaned them out. I asked myself why, since the attack of German measles when she was one, Paula had never wanted to eat. Her only real food was milk chocolate and an occasional egg. The doctor had warned me never to force her to eat and I hadn't, but it worried me to death and everyone else in the family, too. I decided that the priority at the moment was to be together. I couldn't tell Paula that I was trying to earn enough money to get away with her. It wouldn't have been right to unburden my problems on a six-year-old's shoulders.

My absence in Rome had been too long but it had been valuable. It eventually pushed me far enough to write my first novel. But, for the moment, we talked and did simple things at home, or in the village – a fête for the children, a tug of war, taking Paula's pop bottles back to the pub, visiting Eric and Katie Brooks who ran the local post office, or inviting her friends from the farm nearby for tea. Roewen was a peaceful village of hard-working and honourable people. No one locked his car door or his house either. The situation changed a short time later, though, when a council estate was built on the outskirts of the village and a spate of burglaries kept local locksmiths busy for months.

I'd been clearing brambles from the Christmas tree field, when I heard Jess' car arriving on the forecourt of the house. He'd been at his brother's hotel for lunch and was in a state of great excitement. Rushing towards me, he blurted out his good news immediately.

'Mr Clore telephoned me earlier this morning from London. He wants to buy you. He'll pay me £100,000 now and another £50,000 when it's all arranged. I never thought I'd be rich. I shall buy a new car and go to Las Vegas to see Liberace perform.'

I gazed at Jess, who seemed unaware that receiving a takeover bid for your wife was not an everyday occurrence. I tried to understand what had persuaded Charles to do such a thing without asking me if I wished to be sold.

Unaware of my reaction, Jess continued happily, 'He said he wasn't going to do anything behind my back. He's offered me a good deal and he's given me five days to think it over. Paula will be put into Benenden School and he'll give you a place in the country near his stud.'

I went to the kitchen and made tea, staring at Jess' beaming face and feeling very sad and very old, although I was barely out of my twenties. Jess had refused me a divorce three times already, saying that no one would every marry me while he was alive. But now he was willing and even eager to sell me to be the possession, if not the wife, of one of the richest men in the country. I thought of Visconti, whom and I had met in Rome and would come across again in London, who had said so often, 'Write about your life, Elena, write about you.' Could I write a novel? I had the sudden desire to take refuge alone and far away from everyone except Paula, with nothing for company but a block of clean, white paper. If I wrote a novel and it sold, she and I could go away to safety and sanity. I began to dream of a new life and went out to buy a little typewriter in preparation for my bid for freedom.

For a few days, Jess continued to dream of being rich. I asked him again for a divorce, saying that I would make no financial demands at all, other than a small maintenance for Paula. Her school fees were already paid by her godfather. I said I wanted to start again and to take up a writing career. Jess asked if I had someone else and I replied truthfully that I had no one. I just didn't want to be married any more, nor did I want to be sold to the man who'd made the offer. Jess fell silent, which was always a bad sign. Unpredictable as always, Jess suddenly asked me to cut the clematis and honeysuckle that climbed up the front of the house and which had now reached roof level.

'I'll put the stepladder outside for you,' he said, very quietly.

His face was set and he had a distant look in his eyes and I wondered why he had changed the subject. I wanted a divorce, but when I tried to discuss it, he began to look dangerous. I decided it was best to humour him and cut the climbers that might damage the roof. I could discuss divorce when he was feeling more relaxed.

As I approached the ladder, Jess came out of the house, put his keys in the car and threw his overcoat on the back seat. I climbed up the ladder and started cutting tendrils and branches. Behind me, I heard Jess approach, then a funny noise. I turned, wondering what he was doing. Then, without warning, the stepladder collapsed and I fell from the roof on to a solid slate terrace. Jess had cut the cord linking the two sides of the ladder. I cried out for help, shattered to hear the car moving down the drive. Jess had run away to his mother's yet again.

Unable to move, I lay flat on my face. Unimaginable pain moved in waves over me and I must have fainted, because when I woke, I heard the clock in the living room chime eleven. When I had climbed the ladder, it had just chimed ten. Bit by bit, I moved my arms. They were unhurt, my shoulders also but I could not get up because of the pain in my back and the agony in both feet and lower legs. As I couldn't move, I lay there for five hours until Paula arrived alone, for the first time, from school. I explained to her that I'd had a 'little accident' and asked her to be very careful and bring the phone with the long lead from the hall to me on the terrace. She did what I asked and soon help came.

My family asked me, years later, when they were told about this, why I didn't go to the police. Jess was well known from his days on the children's television programmes for the BBC. If I had lodged a complaint for all the different acts of violence that happened each time I asked for a divorce, I knew he would never have worked again and I didn't want that. Strange as it may seem, I stopped feeling angry after each assault – they simply stiffened my resolve to write and get away from Jess. Unfortunately, we don't realise when we're young that injuries like this come back to haunt us when we're old.

Bone scars don't forget. I walk every day and do my ballet barre exercises when I have a bit of energy, so I'm lucky that I can walk, run and most important of all, laugh. That's what's really important.

A short time after this, my mother-in-law was taken to court because Ginger, her dog, had chased sheep. I thought it odd of Ginger, who was the softest dog in the world and believed he was a cat because his basic training had been done by Snowy, the boss-cat of the household. I remembered his taking little kittens in his mouth, copying their mother's actions and walking up and down the terrace behind the matriarch to show everyone that he was a good cat! How proud he had been of the kittens and how they had adored him. That Ginger had chased sheep seemed incomprehensible to me and the news that Sybil was going to move out, having bought a bungalow in the nearby town where Teddy and his wife Joey lived and where there weren't any tempting sheep, was very sad indeed. After detesting each other at the beginning of the marriage, we had succeeded in finding a base for harmony in the house. We'd gone to painting classes together and had our own irreverent jokes. To comfort myself, I put my typewriter on a table, got out a pile of paper and a wad of writing pads and thought that soon I'd start my novel. I had the same thought for months, but never wrote a line.

Often, I looked back on our early days in the house. All had gone well between Sybil and me, the only cloud on the horizon being that one night she had found a bat in her bedroom. It had escaped from the roof space and although not of the Dracula family size, it terrified Sybil, whose insomnia worsened by leaps and bounds. She began to get up at two in the morning, because she could no longer sleep for worrying whether Billy Bat was lurking in a corner. This problem led to one of our most successful joint projects, the double English breakfast.

As Paula was so often ill with bronchial problems, which worried all of us, particularly when the specialists commented that she might not live to the age of ten, there were long periods when she had to have postural drainage three times a day: before school, after school and around one-thirty in the morning. As I only slept four hours a night, this was not too difficult, though it was an uncomfortable procedure for Paula, since she had to be turned upside down with her head towards the floor and then have the base of her lungs tapped so that she would spit out the accumulated phlegm. The problem was that it took time and broke up my nights, so I decided early on to make my first breakfast around two in the morning.

One night, smelling delicious cooking aromas, Sybil wandered into the kitchen, shivering in the cold and wide awake. Realising for the first time that I, too, was a meagre sleeper, she sat at the table and I handed her a plate of eggs and sausage and American hash browns. Then we drank tea and ate toast with home-made rhubarb and apple jam, her favourite. The first breakfast was around two and the second, with Paula, at seven, when we had fruit compôte and Danish pastries made by Sybil. Our first English breakfast became a much loved occasion. Insomnia seemed a positive thing and the fact that Jess had passed from silence to his now incessant chatter, a reason for optimism rather than fear. We were wrong to think that his illness had taken a turn for the better, but we all wanted to hope and for a while we were happy.

Jess had contacted many television companies trying to find work and had not had one reply. Now he no longer tried. He just talked all the time, to himself mostly, in the woods, in the house, or in the car. He talked when we were alone of the people he hated and spent hours waffling on about revenge. Even Sybil became worried about this persistent negativity that seemed at odds with the laughter Jess had once loved to provoke. The only laughter he now caused was with his supreme talent for the musical fart. Paula and I were once passing on the landing when Jess was in the bathroom, when we heard a veritable flute obligato, an anal version, coming from Jess' direction. It went on and on, rising and falling, twirling and turning, ta rum pum pum ta rum boom boom... ti ti ti... eeeee... ah... ah... hup hup ahooooooo! Both of us burst into laughter. I had never heard such a noise before and I haven't heard one since. If Jess had returned to television he could have earned a fortune making sound recordings of his latest effort. I cherished moments like this, when we could laugh together as a family. Jess did try and do his best as a father and I know he was very fond of Paula, but he always tried to keep her in the house and not let her go out because he knew that I would never leave without her.

I had not realised that in Snowdonia it snows from December until the end of February, often even later. I can't bear the cold and was unhappy to think that for three months of the year, in order to use the car, I would have to clear two tyre tracks the whole length of the drive. I did this daily in the snow season, wrapped like a babushka in five pullovers, two pairs of trousers, two or three jackets and with a giant, heavy, woollen stole wrapped around my head and crossed over chest and shoulders.

One day a man drove to the house gates just as I was ending the arduous task and called out to me.

'I'm lost, can you direct me to the house of the magistrate Miss Gee?'

I did so and off he went with a wave. I was thawing out in the house ten minutes later, when the phone rang and Isoline Gee, the magistrate, said, 'Elaine, do come over for coffee.' I adored Isoline and went on foot up and over the hill to her house. She said, 'Take off all those clothes and go into the lounge.' I took off my giant stole, three jackets and one of my pairs of trousers and went to meet her caller, who looked thunderstruck when I shook hands. Isoline laughed delightedly.

'Elaine, this gentleman told me he'd just been directed to

the house by a young woman who weighed at least 20 stone. So much for your snow-clearing outfit!'

Since my refusal to be sold, Jess had become morose. Worried by his constant mood swings, the family doctor finally prevailed upon him to see a psychiatrist. Jess returned from a preliminary consultation furious.

'That fellow is completely mad, mad as a hatter, Elaine. He told me I was talking in a muddled fashion and he couldn't understand a word I said. I shan't go again.'

My heart sank, but I decided to try to cheer Jess up and we went to the pictures, having organised the young daughter of the farm nearby to come and sit with Paula. The film was a comedy and we laughed heartily. Jess ate fish and chips afterwards with his usual HP sauce, talking happily in the car, as I drove home through the dark lanes of the Conway Valley. I told Jess how, sometimes, when Paula was unwell in the night and coughing hard, I used to bundle her up in an eiderdown, carry her out to the car and then take her on a drive, to take her mind and mine off her lung problems. I rather enjoyed those drives. In the dark silence of night, the car headlights often revealed startled owls or bats and sometimes a shy animal out for a stroll in the woods. When Jess finally went to bed, I could hear him talking away in his room. The conversation with himself didn't end until two in the morning.

I sat in bed thinking of the wide-eyed apprehension of Olwen, the young sitter who had guarded Paula. She had heard funny noises in the house during our absence. On investigation, this proved to be Paula snoring! I got up and went to look at my daughter and found her sleeping with a new pair of shoes on her bed.

I loved her so much, I lived in terror of dying and leaving her before I'd taught her to be independent. Paula, herself, admitted when she was older that she could be clingy and rather possessive just as my mother had tried to keep the hooks on me, wanting to possess me for ever. If I made an error later in my handling of Paula's upbringing, it was due to my fear of being like my mother and not letting go, even when she was old enough to do without me. Perhaps I let go too soon and Paula interpreted this as a lack of interest in her. It wasn't that. I just didn't want to be a nuisance mother who considers she is indispensable when she isn't.

In the months that followed my return, Jess tried to get work, but couldn't. The problem was not a lack of talent or ability, but a lack of control. He talked non-stop or not at all and interviews became fiascos. The doctor had tried putting him on Valium or Librium, but both acted on Jess in the opposite way from their normal effect. I became more and more anxious to find a way to be independent. It had such priority in my mind that sometimes I thought of little else except Paula and our life together with the cats and Harold Hare, who often hopped into the kitchen at breakfast time. Sometimes I thought of the doctor's comment on Paula, that if she continued to have chest infections she might not reach the age of ten. This had terrified me and Jess and made us feel guilty for having spoilt her.

When he was home, Jess went every week to a local saleroom to buy things he liked for the house. He had no money and had been warned not to do this any more by his mother and his brother, who had until now paid his bills. Money was scarce and more than once I hid upstairs when bailiffs hammered at the door. We were saved *in extremis* by Teddy, who had the patience of a saint and the generosity of one too. He was now married to his girlfriend of long standing, Joey, whose turn it was to incur Sybil's resentment. I was forbidden to telephone my new sister-in-law, or to visit her often, because Jess and his mother feared some form of mutiny by the two interlopers in the family. Joey was highly intelligent and discreet and soon learned to walk the tightrope of being Sybil's daughter-in-law. It took time, but she managed it and impressed everyone.

Teddy was so happy that nothing upset him, not even Jess' mania for bidding in the saleroom. It upset me, but I could do nothing about his habits. I was busy in any case trying to keep an atmosphere of seeming calm when Paula came home from school. Jess adored his child and even in his most disturbed moments wanted to do his best for her. As always, he photographed Paula and looked at her pictures with adoration. She and Sybil were Jess' objects of true love. I was the person he turned to when he wanted to be reassured or got out of trouble. I was almost twenty years younger than Jess but I had become a kind of reserve mother. Though I had once hoped for a large family I didn't want a baby husband and tried desperately to work out what to do. There seemed little chance of escaping from this maelstrom of perpetual confusion, but I became stronger by the day, biding my time to see if any opportunity arose.

When Charles Clore rang back a week later, Jess told him I didn't wish to be sold. They talked like old friends and it was hard to say who was the more disappointed, Charles, or my husband. As always when he was thwarted, Jess fell silent and began to brood. I was so fed up, I unwisely broached the subject of divorce yet again. Jess looked at me with a strange expression and suggested a picnic in the quarry on the hillside. In better days, we had often gone there together, despite the bad road leading up to it. For the sake of peace, I packed sandwiches and fruit and drove Jess up towards the quarry. The road wound slowly, gaining height in the last few hundred yards. It was easy enough going up, because there was a rock face on the driver's side. Going down there was a precipice. The vertigo that hits me from time to time, due perhaps to the childhood trauma of the lighthouse visit in the Isle of Man, often hit me on the quarry descent.

We ate our sandwiches, drank orange juice and picked armfuls of wild flowers as we always did. Jess barely spoke and still looked at me in a very odd way. Just before returning home, he said, 'Are you really serious about a divorce?' I said I thought it would be best. I refrained from saying that I still wanted more children, if by any miracle I found someone to love. Despite all that had happened, my affection for Jess was deep and I didn't want to hurt him, though I knew hurt would be inevitable if we divorced.

Suddenly, Jess rose and went to the car. I followed, stowed the picnic basket in the boot and began the descent. I was about halfway down when Jess hit me a great resounding punch that burst my nose. I saw blood shoot on to the windscreen and turned to look at him. Further punches followed, then he leapt from the car as I fought to keep from driving over the edge. I could barely see and kept thinking of the lorries that sometimes drove up to the quarry. If I met one of those, I knew I would not survive. The only thing that kept me from panicking was remembering that Paula was due home from school. I drove at a snail's pace to the foot of the mountain and then the short distance to the house. I didn't cry. I didn't even blame Jess, realising that he had had a moment of madness about which he would remember nothing. Yet again, it was another instance of his fragile mental balance I eventually concluded that the loss of his show-business life in London and our enforced period at the hotel had driven him to this state. I pitied him. But my only concern at this moment was to get myself cleaned up, throw away the bloodstained clothes and somehow collect Paula when she left school and take her away before Jess got back to her.

I took a shower and became conscious of a dull throbbing in the lower part of my face. When I looked at myself in the mirror I saw that I had a cut on the right nostril and a swollen nose like a red ball. My left eye had closed. I couldn't move my mouth without intense pain and most of my teeth were wobbling. I rang the doctor and told him what had happened and asked him to meet me at the station to see if he could give me something to reduce the swelling and pain. He did better than that and picked me and then Paula up and took us to the station. As he and I drove down the Plas Yn Roe en route to Llandudno Junction, I heard Jess in the distance shouting the same words over and over again, 'Elaine, I've just killed my mother.' I felt profound pity for Jess, who had finally cracked. But my desire to escape was stronger than any other consideration.

All horrors end and this one did too, but it took a long time. I spent seven months with dentists, who took out a total of eleven broken teeth. Then the Columbia Pictures dentist, who was recommended to me by Theo Cowan – whose PR company I began working for – constructed bridges and caps to cover up the damage. The jaw remained a problem. For ten years, it dislocated every time I laughed, chewed hard or yawned. Finally, one day, I went to see the famous faith healer, George Chapman, with a friend who had booked a consultation. I waited in the car and then Mr Chapman came out with my friend. He called to me and ran a hand over my face about two inches from my right ear. The jaw never went out of joint again. The psychological effect of the violence was a severe loss of confidence and a feeling of disillusionment with life. The only antidote for my condition was my work and so I worked and read and walked miles and made love with some of the men that I met. To me, it seemed a natural thing to do. The Pill was now readily available and I, like many women, felt in control of my body. London was a place of adventure for me and I met some fascinating people and some exasperating ones. While working for Theo Cowan's office, I was asked to look after the film star, Topol, who was appearing in the stage version of *Fiddler on the Roof.* He was a great performer and judging by the length and passion of the standing ovation that the cast received at the end of the opening night, was very impressive.

At a reception in London one evening, a very fresh Tom Jones approached me, he followed me around for a while until his persistence paid off and I stopped to talk to him in an alcove. He had had a couple of hit songs and everyone was aware of him. I found him amusing and liked his Welsh accent and, of course, he was fabulously handsome. Panting like a lap dog, he made his desires clear and I wondered what he would do if for the only time in my life I said yes to a younger man.

He didn't need to be told twice, and drawing a curtain

around us, my skirt was soon around my shoulders and Tom proved that men of Harlech really do achieve glory! This is the one episode in my life where I wonder 'was I mad?' Or was it simply a long-hidden curiosity about young men. However, as we straightened ourselves up, Tom said, 'I didn't know there'd be so many people here tonight,' and I wondered how he knew there were hundreds of guests around.

It was only when he drew the curtain that had been covering our activities that I realised it was entirely transparent and our escapade had probably been seen by dozens of people. I never saw Tom again and after that shock erotica, I went back to elderly elegants.

I kept up a killing, frenetic pace to make sure I didn't stop to think of the past. I had been a fighter during my childhood illness, on the exhausting Bluebells European tour, when I got Fellini to cast me in his film and when Jess knocked seven bells out of me, so I knew I could survive and I willed myself to do so for the sake of my daughter.

First I took a place for us to live in London and put Paula into school. We walked to St George's through Hyde Park each morning and came back the same way in the afternoon. The studio apartment had two tiny divan beds in the living room, a galley kitchen and bathroom. It was too small, but all I could afford and we were happy together, because life was calmer. For me, it was a tiny paradise until one day I opened the door and found Jess on the other side. He said he didn't like living in the house without his mother and without me, so he was going to live with us. 'I shall sleep on the floor,' he said, 'as there isn't anywhere else.' Afraid of provoking him to violence, I simply said he could stay the night but that three people could not live in such a small space. Then I went to pick up Paula from school. I was shaking from head to toe with every emotion in the book – anger, shock, fear and above all the now insurmountable desire to break away from the past.

Leaving the park, I crossed by the Dorchester and went to the school. Paula was just coming out. She was as white as a sheet and seemed short of breath. I picked her up in my arms, hailed a taxi and went immediately back to the apartment. The doctor arrived a few minutes later, an impressive gentleman in a dark jacket and grey, striped trousers. After examining Paula, he said she had pneumonia, handed me a prescription and said she must drink as much as possible. He would return first thing in the morning.

All the known medicaments for pneumonia didn't work on Paula, who became worse and worse. A specialist was called in and an atypical pneumonia diagnosed. Finally, Paula, who had a temperature of over 100 looked at me and said, 'Am I dying, Mummy?' and I replied, 'Not if I can help it.'

I rang Jess' family and mine and asked everyone to say a

prayer for Paula. If God exists, I felt sure he would help her. Then I took her into my bed and she crawled like a little animal to lie flat, her body on mine, her chest on mine. I was never as hot in my life, but I didn't dare move in case a change of position upset her. Hours passed. I imagined death lurking in every corner of the room. Then, at dawn, Paula opened her eyes and said, 'I could eat some boiled potatoes.' I leaped up, put some on to cook, took her temperature and found it normal. It was, after the day of Paula's birth, the very best day of my life and I sang like thunder for hours.

Probably as a result of my singing, Jess voluntarily entered the York Clinic at Guy's Hospital as a patient of David Stafford Clark, probably England's most renowned psychiatrist. He was a small, elegant man who wrote poetry, but I had difficulty establishing a relationship with him because his eyes appeared to be covered with a curious, gelatinous film, like a fish's. I like looking in to people's eyes and if I can't see them, it's difficult for me to assess them. I only met Dr Stafford Clark twice, when he asked me to verify Jess' responses to his questions. His eventual diagnosis was that Jess was a manic depressive with schizophrenic tendencies.

Paula was eight by the time she had got over her illness and weighed what a normal child of four should weigh. But, for the first time since the age of one, she ate and ate and ate, sometimes four or five cooked meals a day. At first, she stayed with me, then she went back to Wales to convalesce at her uncle and aunt's when I became ill with a chest infection. For three weeks, I waited for Max and Bluma Trell to arrive from New York to take over our home. They were coming to spend a year's sabbatical in England and I was so happy to see them.

One the day of their arrival, I invited them to meet my favourite man, Guy the Gorilla from London Zoo. I often used to go and see Guy because he was magnificent and had such a mysterious look in his eyes I was bewitched. On approaching his cage with the Trells, I saw that Guy had a particularly intense look on his face. 'Hello my beauty,' I said, 'how are you today?'

I heard Bluma bark out an order: 'Come along, dear, time to go!'

But Guy was so intent, his eyes on mine, that I stayed, staring in awe at his dark, brooding face. Finally Max Trell came, took me by the arm and dragged me away. I was a bit annoyed and disappointed that they hadn't adored Guy as I did. Then Max turned to me and said in his marvellous Brooklyn accent, 'Goddamn it, Elaine, do you have to stand as close as that when the gorilla's masturbating. Bluma and I near died of embarrassment!'

I'd been so enthralled by the look in Guy's eyes that I hadn't noticed the rest.

That evening a famous English writer, Wolf Mankowitz, whom I had met in Theo Cowan's office, invited me to dinner and I told him that I wanted to write a book.

Writers get very tired of hearing about would-be writers' dreams and Wolf replied, 'If you want to write write, but don't talk about it!' I thought, 'I will, too. I shall start the moment I get home.' As it eventually turned out, Wolf eventually read my first book and found me an agent in London, but by chance, a few weeks afterwards, I read about an editor in a Sunday paper, who was considered unconventional and who believed very much in publicising his authors. As the rather prestigious agent that Wolf had recommended to me had had some rejections, I wrote to this editor to ask if he would read my book and, after we met, he offered me a contract with his company, the New English Library.

Paula could not go to school for the first term after we returned to Wales in case she caught another infection. This was good news for both of us and we recommenced precious routines – going for walks in the woods, Paula playing with the cats, or whatever animal she could find. She was wonderful with all of them. At this time, I seemed to spend hours each day cooking up a storm to try to satisfy her new-found appetite. And every evening, after Paula went to bed, I sat in front of a white notepad trying to write. I forced myself to sit for two hours, waiting for the nerve to write something, anything. A week passed, two, three, four and not a word on the paper. Tears were very near, but I'm incapable of giving up when I want to do something. Then, one day, I was making tea in the kitchen when I found a tiny lustre pot my grandmother had given me when I was small. On the side there was a Victorian rhyme, banal as they so often are, but the banal little poem made me write. It said,

> 'You can if you think you can, that's half the
> battle won.
> Remember it whenever there's a big task to be
> done.
> To say you can't when effort calls means just
> that you've lost heart.
> You're asking for defeat before you've even made
> a start.'

In the morning I rushed upstairs to the office and took out the ominously empty notepad and wrote: 'I should begin this story somewhere. My name is Andrea, Andrea Webster. I'm sure you know the name...

Then, out of the corner of my eye, I saw Paula arrive with a tray of tea and biscuits and I told her joyfully that I'd started the book. We drank our tea and ate the biscuits and then took the cats for their morning adventure. I'd only written a few words, but I was sure I could finish the novel. As I had no idea how to write narrative, I wrote the entire novel in the first person and present tense, which the Americans considered avant garde. Writing in the first person, in the present tense is technically difficult, but I didn't realise that. They say that ignorance is bliss and I was a five-star ignoramus when it came to writing. I knew only that I wanted to write, earn a living and go far away with Paula. Watching her running through the woods with the cats I was motivated as never before to finish the novel. We all have to have the mental and physical force to function in difficult circumstances. I had Paula. I also had the experience of having survived a childhood that was not at all like most other people's. I was lucky. I'd written my first two phrases and I had enough strength of character to go on.

The next morning, when I saw the white notepad, I was struck, yet again, by the fear of being unable to write. In all, this fear lasted seven years, after which I decided that if I wanted to write, I could, and no excuses were valid. In the meantime, I attacked the empty sheet and filled it. Then I filled another. I was thinking with deep satisfaction that perhaps someday, in twenty years' time, I would be a real writer.

CHAPTER FIFTEEN

Jess left the York Clinic and began again to try to find work. He never talked about his treatment in the clinic and I knew very little having met David Stafford Clark so briefly. I remembered the first meeting with him because of his eyes. He was charming, but uncommunicative. I remember the second because I had been to the British Museum's reading room to search out an early work of poetry by him and had found an interesting quatrain 'Retrospection' which I felt held the key to part of the man. When I told Dr Stafford Clark that I had read his poems and mentioned the four lines of 'Retrospection', I had what was probably the only spontaneous reaction he had shown a visitor in many years. It was displeasure.

I mentioned on this occasion the fact that Jess had the

habit of saying to people that he was writing a book and that his wife was looking for work in television, in other words reversing the roles. The doctor's response was, 'Well, he obviously finds it easier to be you than to be himself.'

I didn't ask many questions. The labyrinthine processes of the mind are too complicated for even the most brilliant researchers. I just wanted to know if Jess would get better, but of course no one could tell me that.

When Jess received no replies to his letters of application for work, Sybil asked me to do something to help. I went to see her and she said, 'There must be something wrong with his letters that he never gets a reply. You write one for him.' So I wrote a letter of application for work for myself to Donald Baverstock of Yorkshire Television (YTV).

The letter was unconventional, along the lines of 'They say you're a difficult bastard to work with...' I had an immediate reply and was interviewed shortly afterwards by the producer Tony Essex. Through him I met Mr Baverstock, a brilliant, fiery, ex-BBC producer of impressive reputation and knock-out intellect. He teased me that he was going to frame my letter and put it on the wall. Eventually, Tony Essex offered me a programme that involved touring old museums and reconstructed ancient houses to describe how people used to live. At the last moment, I said that due to my daughter's health problems I couldn't do it, but that my husband Jess Yates could. An interview was arranged for Jess and I returned home to try to teach him in a week how to control his desire to talk all the time. It was almost impossible, but Jess was so pathetically anxious to work, he really tried. His natural charm and perfect ease on camera did the rest and he was given a contract with YTV. He moved to Leeds shortly after his contract was signed and I returned to trying to write my novel.

It finally took me a year to write 35,000 words, each sentence the product of sweated labour and the cause of nightmares every night. The book, entitled *The Performer*, was sold in the UK and then in the USA. I was very pleased, but somehow I still didn't feel I was a writer. On the strength of it, though, I acquired an American literary agent recommended by the author Geoffrey Bocca, who told me to get started on a second novel.

I went back to Wales and wrote all day while Paula was at school, correcting and typing out what I'd written once Paula was asleep in the evening. I made so many errors, I despaired of ever 'becoming a real writer', forgetting that I had already been published.

My days of writing were punctuated by Jess' famous calls for advice. Sometimes he telephoned two or three times. Once, when the family doctor was present, he called ten or eleven times at intervals of five to ten minutes.

Then, one weekend, Jess came home in a state of high anxiety.

'Donald Baverstock wants a religious programme for a Sunday slot that isn't like all the other religious programmes. He wants high viewing figures. I don't ever remember a religious programme that folk wanted to watch. Think of something – it's urgent – then type the format out for me to take back with me tomorrow evening. I'm seeing him on Monday morning.'

I've always found religious programmes horribly boring because of miserable-faced, warbling vicars. So I wrote down the details of what I considered an entertaining Sunday programme. Actors would read the Bible, famous musicians, opera singers or rock stars could sing hymns or play something with special meaning for them. Jess loved it and rushed back to Leeds on Sunday afternoon.

At nine-thirty on Monday he rang me.

'For God's sake Elaine, you didn't put a title on the format. Donald Baverstock wants one immediately, what shall I say?'

'How about *Stars on Sunday*?' I replied.

'Oh I like it,' he said and rang off.

At five o'clock that evening, an ecstatic Jess rang me. I have never forgotten the call, which stunned me but still made me laugh. Jess said, 'I've had a wonderful idea for a religious programme. I put it to Donald Baverstock this morning and he's proposed an extension of my contract. I shall front the programme and I've called it *Stars on Sunday*.' I replied with a certain acerbity that I had written the format for him on Sunday and had proposed the title that very morning. Jess laughed like a child.

'Oh yes, I'd forgotten it was you.'

I said that I wasn't asking him to pay me for what I'd

written but I did want a credit for the original idea. I never got one. Jess couldn't bear to admit that I had written the format, or any other material that I wrote for him. After that, success came for Jess. The success was of such magnitude that it changed him and not for the better. He still rang between three and ten times a day and from time to time came to Plas Yn Roe when he needed a new idea. I never asked to be paid for the ideas but always asked if he could give me a credit – 'from an original idea by Helene Thornton'. He never did.

YTV once paid me an ex-gratia payment of £450 when it was discovered that Jess had stolen the carbon copy of a children's book that I was working on, *The CV Wolf Stories*, and had had puppets made for each character with a view to making a children's series. These stories were the bedtime laughter makers for Paula and concerned a wolf family who lived in a log cabin in our woods. I took the cheque and didn't complain. I preferred Jess working far away and happy if I could continue writing. The first novel had sold well enough to warrant a second one. I was well advanced on that one, too. When the weather forecaster announced that all the signs indicated that we would have a very hard winter, I decided to take Paula out to Malta, where we stayed for a year and where I finished and revised the second novel, *Not for Beginners*, for which I already had a contract with Pocket Books who were part of Simon & Schuster, one of the large US publishing houses. It eventually sold over 200,000 copies. I still wrote in the first person, in the present tense and produced four novels like that before I finally learned to write in a narrative style for a series of historical novels on the lives of interesting but unknown women of the past.

Malta was hot and often windy. It didn't rain between April and October, but the year we were there it had still not rained by the third week in November. The streets, polished by months of dust and beach sand, became as slippery as ice rinks which made walking a hazard. One day, I was returning from looking at houses to rent when I missed my footing on a bend on the way back to our hotel. When I fall it's like the tower of Pisa coming down, so I grabbed the nearest solid object to try to break the fall. The nearest solid object was the imposing head of a small man coming in the opposite direction. We fell to the ground together. He rose, brushed himself down and looked angrily at me from his full height of 5 feet 3 inches. Then, without a word, he walked away and entered a house nearby. I hurried to the hotel and forgot about him.

I signed the lease on the house I'd chosen and we moved in. Paula loved Malta and the fact that she had my undivided attention (at last!). She was enrolled in a school nearby and I began learning the routines of this fascinating island. My neighbours taught me how and what to buy from the fish vendor who came every day. They taught me to make octopus soup with lemon and rice and also

aubergines stuffed with *lampuka* (dolphin). They told me
not to shed tears for the poor old man with the bent back
who collected the refuse each morning. I cried anyway.
After delivering Paula to school, I wrote and then, if all
went well, I would relax by painting knights of Malta in
the only light place in the house, the square entrance hall
with its glass front door. The neighbours often watched,
pressing their noses against the glass. After lunch, I swam
at the nearby hotel and corrected what I'd written earlier
until it was time to collect Paula from school. Sometimes,
we returned to the hotel to swim, but in mid-winter we
went to the house and prepared dinner, or went shopping
in the centre of Sliema. Paula was a very good companion,
always making me laugh, especially when she knew I was
not supposed to laugh. While she slept, I typed again, or
corrected my endless writing errors.

I was painting one morning when a young man came
and knocked at the glass window. When I opened it he
said, 'I'd like to see your pictures.' I replied that I didn't sell
my pictures, but he walked in, looked briefly around and
said, 'My father will want one of those.' Then he thanked
me and left.

I was used to the neighbours standing at the window
watching me work, but not to people arriving and
earmarking pictures that weren't for sale. Collage and
painting have always been my escape routes from the
tensions of day-to-day existence and a professional
novelist's life. I have one particular collage in my home in

France that I made for Paula at her request. It's bronze and gold in colour with a doll's face at the centre. To me, it represents childhood and the child that is always inside us. Below is the opening line of a story, which reads, 'Once upon a time, there was a little girl who lived in a big house at the top of a hill…' I had intended to give it to Paula, but the right opportunity never arose.

Only recently have I shown my work, due to an enforced rest from writing that unexpectedly lasted twelve years, when I spent time looking after my seriously ill French husband. In France, explanations of the work in my sing-song accent have caused much hilarity and contributed to a festive atmosphere in my own private exhibitions. It's not unknown for some regulars to arrive with a bottle of champagne and to sit down in the hall to enjoy it. A few years ago, I showed in London for the marvelously charismatic Jean Luc Aeby, who owned the Sydney House hotel in London who often put on art exhibtions. I've also become something of a regular at the Salon de Collage in Paris and I am booked to show in Milan and at the Musée de Collage in Burgundy.

One night there was a knock at the door. I looked at the clock and saw it was nine in the evening. I was typing and dressed in an old pair of satin knickers and a rose kimono. I went to the door and saw the tiny man I had knocked over when falling in the street the month previously. Opening the door, I asked what he wanted.

'I've come to see the pictures. My son liked them very

much.' He entered as if he owned the place, looked around and unhooked two which he handed to his chauffeur. Then, with a charming smile, he thanked me and said he would send someone round with a cheque. On trying to descend the three steps in the house in the pitch dark, he missed his footing and fell.

I said, 'Are you hurt? It's really a disgrace that the government can't light all the streets in a town as important as Sliema.'

He looked hard at me and then walked to his car and was driven away. I closed the door and went back to my typing. The man was a gentleman, not a criminal and I knew he would keep his word, but what an odd thing to do to come at night in the darkness to take pictures that I had already said weren't for sale. I stood in the hall for some time looking at the pictures and thinking that as I could only do one thing at a time I must concentrate on the writing and try to do better.

At the crack of dawn the inhabitants of the street were awakened by the sound of a pneumatic drill operating directly outside my house. I took a shower, got Paula ready for school and then went outside to see my neighbour and teacher of Maltese ways to ask her what was happening. She came over, her face wreathed in smiles, to thank me.

'Why are you thanking me?' I asked.

'We've been asking for so long for lights to be put in this street, but no one ever came. Then, last night, when the prime minister fell on your stairs you told him it was a pity the government couldn't light the streets of the town. So he sent men over to install lamps in the street.'

Things were going smoothly, until my mother arrived for her summer 1969 holiday in Malta. She stayed in an hotel because there was only one bedroom in my tiny house. She then hired a car so I could drive her around the island. She was a terrible back-seat driver and regularly shouted instructions – 'There's a bus coming!' 'The traffic lights are red!' Once, she leaped out of the car on the precipitous edge of a cliff where I had driven because the road sign had said Beach Road. What it didn't say was that the road was the same width as the car and ended some 100 yards on in a sheer drop of immense dimension that necessitated a parachute to reach the beach. I backed up all the way to the road and Paula made me laugh far too much, which enraged Gertrude, who found it impossible to laugh at herself. A week later, I was relieved to return the car to the garage. Then Gertrude came to tea and announced that she had bought a little house not far from Valletta. I asked her why. Was it her intention to come and live in Malta?

'No,' she replied, 'I just liked the look of it so I bought it.'

Since my father's death some seven years previously, Gertrude had been alone and had dreamed year after year of travelling the world, but she was not rich enough to do so. Then, one of my father's friends asked her to marry him. Gertrude refused in case he tried to assert his conjugal rights. The gentleman was over eighty, but Gertrude didn't want to take the risk of any hanky panky. So in love with her was he that he had accompanied her to Malta but had had to return to England because it was too hot for his bad heart. Before leaving, he had bought my mother the tiny house, which she showed me before asking me to drive her into Valletta to buy a stove, table, chairs, a bed and a fridge.

Like her grandfather, my mum loved buying houses and the cheaper the better. After the purchase, she painted everything in sight with white paint and then usually re-sold the house at a profit. She was, in her way, a very astute lady and had rarely made an error. In Malta, however, in a primitive village near Valletta, out of time and far from her usual cast-iron routines, I was very afraid of unexpected problems. Despite her usual fear of anything 'foreign', Mum went ahead despite my advice. She never did like advice.

The house-warming party was memorable, lunch for eight on the terrace under a pergola heavy with scented jasmine. I had made a salad buffet and cooked a very large white-fleshed fish that I told Trudie was halibut, which was a lie, but if I'd said dolphin she would have vomited. The guests drank Maltese white wine; I drank bottled water, as the local wine seemed to me good only for rust removal or cleaning out the drains.

Everything was going well. Mother was flushed with delight at her new acquisition and the pretty buffet and the scent of her very own pergola. Then, as she raised the knife to serve a giant sultana pastry she had made, she sensed movement above her head. I was smiling across the table at her when, to my horror, mother changed colour from ruddy rose to chalky white. She was looking fixedly upwards but seemed unable to speak. Afraid she had had a stroke, I leapt up and ran to her side. My sudden movement frightened the gecko perched overhead on one of the pergola rails, peacefully eating flies and he fell on to the table, bolted and then climbed back up again. From his place in the sun, he surveyed everyone with an unblinking, basilisk gaze.

One of the guests was the lawyer who had just arranged the purchase of the house for my mother. Seeing her catatonic state he turned to me.

'Shall I call a doctor, Helene?'

My mother croaked, 'Crocodile!'

Paula began to hoot with laughter and had to be taken for a walk by a woman friend. The lawyer rose, increasingly agitated, as Mother ran in a panic into the house, eyes rolling, breath rasping from her lungs. Once in her chair, she sobbed uncontrollably, but could say nothing except 'Crocodile! Crocodile!'

I made tea, the English remedy for everything stressful. Then I tried to explain to mother that the 'crocodile' was a gecko, a lizard who liked nothing better than sitting in the sun eating flies. He did not eat people. In fact, he preferred not to see them at all and usually slept all day. Mother blinked and then motioned to the lawyer.

'Hotel Phoenicia and sell the house.'

'But, madame, you only just bought it.'

'Sell! Sell! Hotel Phoenicia.'

I explained to the guests that I was going to drive Gertrude to the Hotel Phoenicia in Valletta. In that hallowed colonial enclave, at least in theory, she would be safe from geckos, crocodiles and all things foreign. One of the men present, very taken by the house, particularly the pergola, began negotiating with the lawyer to buy.

I drove Mum to the hotel, saw her to her room, ordered afternoon tea with Madeira cake and said I would return in the evening. She was still very pale and couldn't understand how anyone could stay on an island full of 'prehistoric animals' that fell on the table during lunch.

Returning to the guests, we finished the pastry Mum had made, threw out her weak coffee and enjoyed the lawyer's version of Turkish coffee. Each guest told a story based on the gigantic size of Maltese fauna; the centipedes of Olympian dimension, the geckos often perched on the ceilings of hotel rooms and mistaken by British tourists for baby crocodiles, and the pretty little 'kitten' my daughter had wanted to stroke on the promenade in Sliema, who turned out to be King Rat. The guests were all Maltese, except for Agnes, an American army wife capable of karate-chopping anything from a bear to a four-star general. At the army base in Arizona, where she had lived for years, she was responsible for teaching new wives how to kill rattlesnakes. Still amazed by my mother's histrionics, Agnes leaned across the table.

'What's your mum really going to do, Helene?'

'Sell the house and leave. She'll not go outside the hotel until she's signed the deed of sale.'

The lawyer shook his head in perplexity.

'I have never met such a person, not even among the British who are a very strange race.' Three days later, one of the lunch guests bought mother's house at a bargain price. He was buying a property for each of his seven grandchildren and was thrilled by the deal. Mother lost money but very little and didn't care too much. After the signing, she asked me to drive her to the airport. Her bags were already in the car. There remained only one thing to do. I watched in horror as she inspected every inch of the interior 'in case of dangerous animals'. Then she sprayed it with Shelltox, which effectively stopped me breathing and necessitated a long delay to clear the air.

At the airport, Gertrude was gracious with everyone except me. Before passing through to the departure lounge, she said goodbye, kissed me sadly and looked me in the eye with regret.

'I don't know why you're like you are, Elaine. You aren't at all British, always eating unidentifiable things, talking foreign languages and living in places only fit for savages. No one in our family has ever been so odd.'

And with that, she walked away on her white plastic shoes to the departure lounge and I went out to the little hired car, shaking my head at the adjective she had used. Odd. Mother was the only person I ever met who wore her beautiful mink coat with white, plastic shoes. The phobia of her life had always been frogs, now joined by geckos and the entire animal population of Malta and all places east of England. She believed learning languages to be unpatriotic, but had once called me from Naples to ask me to explain her symptoms to the Italian doctor who had been called. And *she* considered *me* odd? No matter.

Our routines were fun in Malta. While Paula was at school, I sometimes went to eat a plate of pasta in the nearby hotel, where the manager let me swim. The chef showed me his way with very thin spaghetti and his sauces that were so delicious and so simple, with black olives, anchovies and tomato or cream and fresh parmesan. I still make them his way, but never as well as he did.

Often I drove Paula to the ancient fortress city of Mdina, so that we could sit in the twilight on the warm stone steps watching as the domes and spires turned crimson in the sunset. They call Petra 'a rose-red city half as old as time'. For me, Mdina was even better. It was quite simply one of the few unforgettable places I ever visited. Twilight was cerise and then, slowly, a deep violet turning midnight blue as crenellated walls that had withstood siege and strife for centuries became dark silhouettes awaiting the dawn. I think of it still. Some people are addicted to drink or drugs. I'm addicted to beauty and the unreal atmosphere that comes at sunset and again, just before dawn, when the sun rises and life begins again. And often, at sunset, I remember the day when Paula said, 'This is my favourite place of all, Mummy, because when we come here we're so happy and England is so far away.'

The Maltese prime minister continued his interest in me. He was a gentleman of the old school, deeply intelligent and admirable, but also a little irreverent, which I liked. But I wanted nothing from him except his company. However, when the prime minister began talking of marriage, I knew it was time to leave Malta. He was already married, but separated at that time and so was I. I saw him twice on my return to England. The first time curiosity got the better of him and he arrived wanting to see my mother's house, which I had told him reached a quite spectacular level of bad taste. 'I don't believe that she puts those colours all together in one room. I want to see it. I shall pay my respects to your mother, invite you both to lunch and then I'll return to the Prime Minister's Conference in London.'

I drove him to my mother's house, having warned her days before. Gertrude was ready in her lounge, with its cobalt carpet patterned with giant sunflowers. The three-piece suite was gold and orange and the flowers that decorated the room were red and white imitation dahlias. She brought out some beautiful, cut-glass sherry schooners and served everything in a perfect way. The prime minister rose to look at the garden, and came face to face with a wall of purple curtains. I saw him close his eyes and take a deep breath. Then he turned, impassive, and said, 'You have some wonderful red geraniums.' It wasn't for nothing that my mother considered him the most elegant gentleman she'd ever met. I thought so, too.

Paula looked different after our return from Malta. She was no longer the emaciated wraith that she had been after her illness and for the first time she seemed really well. Jess' work at Yorkshire Television was going well, though he was easily unnerved by even the slightest opposition. He was lucky to have Donald Baverstock as his boss and a man of quality, George Ward Thomas, as managing director. I felt Jess had solid support at the moment in his life when he needed it. I was not in agreement with his view, shared by his mother and most of the family, that Paula should not be told that Jess and I were separated. I was angry when he kept threatening to ask for custody of Paula if I tried to force a divorce. And so things went on as they had done for years and Paula and I went to Leeds for the YTV Christmas celebrations 'to keep up appearances'. I had no idea that Jess was living with someone else at the time, or I would have avoided such ridiculous charades. I wouldn't have been angry. Jess was Jess and he and I had been through a lot together, though our real separation of minds had come years previously.

Almost ten years after our separation, the law in England changed and divorce without consent was made possible. Jess immediately agreed to a divorce by mutual consent, which seemed odd to me, having waited for ten years to be free. I didn't go to court for the divorce hearing, though I saw Jess shortly beforehand, a meeting that had a profound effect on me and my outlook on life. After eighteen years of marriage, he said solemnly, 'I have always loved you. I still love you and I'll love you till the end of my life. But now you've insisted on the divorce, I shall destroy you. I'll make your daughter hate you and your mother disown you.'

Jess' words were a tragic epitaph for a marriage that had started in high comedy and run the gamut of powerful dramas including near tragedy. Having made his statement, Jess walked away, his shoulders hunched and I watched him go, incredulous, saddened and disillusioned by his words. I had tried so hard to teach him that revenge, like hate, is self-destructive. On a day when I should have felt happy, free and ready to take up a new life, instead I felt crushed at the thought that Jess was going to do his utmost to wreak revenge on me.

We didn't meet again until the day of Paula and Bob's wedding. I later learned that he visited my mother and told her she was going to be poisoned for her money. Gertrude had always been paranoid and this information provoked her to change her will. She hated Jess, but such was his talent as a liar, she believed his story. If ever I kill someone, it won't be the coward's way with poison. It could only happen defending those I love or myself. Jess' lies brought the first part of his threat to fruition.

I never succeeded in discovering what he did to make

Paula change her attitude towards me. It happened when she was at sixth-form college in Oxford, where Jess had the help of a gentleman he had known since their youth and of whom he once said, 'He's the only man I ever loved and he's the only man I ever fucked.' Jess was such a liar, I never knew whether to believe him. As for the young man, he was charming and unfailingly kind to me, so I've never pursued the matter further. But Paula became rather distant. She came home one weekend and said, 'I've lost all my confidence, Mummy.' She wouldn't explain why and spent all her time sitting staring at her shoes. All the affection and encouragement I could show her were as nothing. I even made her special Paula pizzas, but she would not eat them. It was the first of a number of differences that I noticed in her.

A couple of years after the divorce, I was told that Jess had taken on a journalist to write a 'revenge book' to ruin me and punish me for the divorce. I rang Jess and asked him to control his desire for revenge for reasons linked with one of my friends. The book was never published, though no doubt it will surface someday. I hope the journalist who ghosted it realised that Jess and the truth remained for ever total strangers. Jess was a champion hater, which proves, perhaps, that when he loved, he loved too much.

I was once interviewed by a young journalist, called Paul Dacre (now editor of the *Daily Mail*). He was quite unlike any other member of the press I had ever met and I never forgot him. One of his questions was, what would I put on my own epitaph? If he had asked me to write something for Jess or Paula, I could have done it, but trying to think of something for me was more than I could manage. Jess said afterwards, 'I shall put Shakespeare's words about Cleopatra on your tombstone: "A lass unparalleled".' His words made me cry buckets for days.

Writing all this, I see the contradictions of the man, but I don't understand them. For my part, I prefer to forget how he lied and how everyone believed his lies as they did, later, believe Paula's. I'm happier remembering one of our later meetings, when I arrived from France for the marriage of Paula and Bob. Jess was playing the organ in the hall. Paula and Bob looked tense to say the least and I was told later that they were expecting us to do fifteen rounds at Madison Square Gardens that day. Instead, I listened to Jess playing. Then, I said, 'Shall we go to the town for afternoon tea?'

He replied, 'That sounds like a good idea.'

And off we went, with me driving because Jess had a vexing habit of forgetting which side of the road he was on. And we had a lovely time.

Some things are, perhaps, for always.

PART THREE

GLIMPSES OF FRIENDS, ENEMIES, PLACES AND TRAINS

I'll walk where my own nature would be leading
It vexes me to choose another guide
Where the grey flocks in ferny glens are feeding
Where the wild wind blows on the mountain side.

EMILY BRONTE, 1818-1848, *STANZA*

CHAPTER SIXTEEN

One day in Rome when I had no work call, I was looking in a boutique window, drooling over a wonderful black dress and an even more spectacular red one, when I saw the reflection of a man behind me. He spoke in a subtle but commanding way. 'The red one is perfect for you.'

Thinking it was just another man trying to pick me up, I didn't turn round or reply but instead went into the boutique and asked to try on the black dress. I had dyed auburn hair then and couldn't imagine myself in red. The black dress made me look like a Sicilian widow. Hurriedly, I asked for the red. It was lovely and I bought it and tripped happily out, coming face to face with the wondrously stylish gentleman who'd given the advice.

He said, 'I hope you're free for lunch.'

'Thank you, yes.'

Face to face with the man, I realised at once that it was Luchino Visconti, the film director. He asked questions by the dozen; not personal questions like journalists do, but more subtle enquiries that demanded opinions and reactions. The meal was lovely, but I hardly dared eat, as each minute was more surprising than the last. Visconti ordered a coffee for me and said, 'I often come here. I like to watch you cross the Via Veneto. No one crosses it like you. I don't know how you find the courage to just step out and force everyone to put their brakes on. And yesterday, when you took Noel Coward by the arm and led him across I nearly applauded. He's very fragile, isn't he?'

We discussed Mr Coward, who, in his old age, had seemed none too certain how to cross the Via Veneto without ending up as flat as a slice of salami.

At the end of the lunch, Visconti wrote an address on the menu and said, 'If you're free, come for the weekend.' He had a house in the country far from the water rationing in the centre of Rome, so I was very happy to accept.

I arrived by taxi and found a country house with highly organised staff. Visconti was in the garden, dressed in tweed trousers in spite of the heat. I told him he looked like a Scottish gardener. He spoke as if we were old friends.

'We're going to dress for dinner. You're wearing a dress in the eighteenth-century style. I chose it to put another of my guests at ease. She's always dressed like something out of an Edgar Allan Poe novel, even when she goes to the cinema.'

A bit astounded by the idea, I said nothing because I was unsure what to say. When I went to my room, I found an ivory satin dress trimmed with two colours of green ribbon. One of the maids put my long hair up in a plait around my head before I went down to meet the other guests – two beautiful young men and a marvellously baroque, titled Roman, who was all in black, apart from a ruby hanging from a chain around her neck. It was so large that I thought she probably used it to knock out potential attackers.

The atmosphere was relaxed but formal, fantastic, but appropriate for Visconti, who regaled us with stories of his youth. At a certain moment, he asked me to tell a story about my childhood and, when I recounted the cemetery incident that opens this book, he leaned forward and said, 'But how did you know what to do when you were so young?'

And I thought about that and realised that I'd been programmed almost entirely by my grandparents. We all discussed age and the titled lady laughed until she cried at my stories about Max and Bluma Trell and Guy the Gorilla. The hours passed, the candles flickered and the silence outside was tangible.

When the guests had gone, Visconti and I sat for a long time in the moonlight on the colonnaded terrace, chatting about everything. He was the only man in my life, apart from Jess, with whom I had an immediate understanding without a word being said, though many words were said in our friendship and all of Visconti's taught me invaluable, if invisible, lessons for the future.

He told me that my childhood and perhaps heredity had made me different, with a view on life that was unusual. Never feel the need to apologise for being different, he said. The most important thing he told me was that each of us can guard the citadel of our inner self from outside interference. Only our exterior, often unreal in comparison with the interior, is available to the watchers, the tricksters and those who need to destroy.

I never saw Visconti again after I left Rome. We were never lovers, but we were drawn to each other. When I stayed with him, Visconti got up earlier than was his habit so that we could walk arm in arm together in the garden. He was, I think, amused by my huge appetite – I ate enough for six at breakfast times – and he loved hearing about my childhood breakfasts with my grandfather when we toasted bread over the fire.

Visconti wrote me one priceless letter five years before his death, 'Today I thought of you, because I saw the dress you wore the first time you came to stay. I am not at all well, but am still a beautiful boy as you called me. I wish you were here to make me laugh.'

The letter disappeared with just about every other souvenir of my past in a series of burglaries that took place after I had been living in Ireland and had decided to move to France. The first burglary was made on my cousin's garage where I was storing some belongings. Then, a second took place in Kent, where I had moved more of my things, so I dispersed everything to various places, giving Paula nearly seventy boxes of books and objects that she liked. However, I was robbed again when I moved to France. Thieves came down from the roof to my bedroom and stole a number of personal papers and legal documents. I immediately had steel doors fitted.

TWO TRAIN TALES

Although I have travelled to many countries, I have probably seen more of Europe than anywhere else. I have always been a train fan since childhood, so the Orient Express was high on my list of priorities and I took it more than once. Nowadays, the Orient Express is a luxurious, romantic fantasy for honeymooners and train lovers, based on novelists' descriptions of the legendary train. Sadly, the real Orient Express, in its final years, was only an echo of what it had been. There was no longer an elegant restaurant car and the cabins were comfortable but shabby. The night stewards remained marvellous, though, advising passengers who arrived, unaware of the lack of food on the train, to 'run to the vendor at the next station and buy some salami or a chicken and bread and then run back. If you don't run fast you will be left on the platform'.

In spite of its shortcomings, though, I remember taking

it from Belgrade to Paris and returning twenty-four hours later to Belgrade. I went specially to buy black silk tights from Repetto in the rue de la Paix, a luxury unobtainable in the Yugoslav capital. I bought my ticket at Putnik, the State travel agency and when I asked if I would need any visas, I was told no, nothing at all. In case of hunger pangs, I bought some stale sandwiches with an uncertain filling, some bottled water and a bag of not very ripe apples. Then I embarked.

I was sound asleep when someone started hammering at the door and shouting 'Passport'. I put on a pareo, opened the door and handed over my passport to the Italian frontier police.

'Where is your visa to enter Italy?' the leader enquired.

'Putnik told me that I don't need a visa. I'm British and that is a British passport.'

'If you don't have a visa, you will have to leave the train.'

Peering into the darkness outside the window, I saw nothing but black emptiness. There were no sounds but the distant barking of a dog. Then I said my favourite word. 'No!'

The guard ordered me to get dressed and leave the train. '*No!*'

He dragged me outside my berth pareo-clad and ordered his companion to pack my bag. I shouted so loud they must have heard me in Clapham Junction. The passengers who dared peered out of their cabins into the corridor, then closed their doors again. I knew only one thing: I would not be put off the train in the middle of the night, undressed and without a map or any idea of where I was. Both guards now tried to drag me to the door, but I'd taken hold of a metal rail and short of knocking me out there was little they could do. I continued to roar like Leo the MGM lion.

At that moment, a man stepped out of a sleeper at the far end of the carriage and called to the guards. As he strode towards them, he spoke perfect Italian and in short sharp phrases told them to get out and belt up. Then he carried my bag back to the cabin, indicated for me to go inside and said in English. 'I am Mirja's friend. Those fools at Putnik think it's fun to make problems like this for foreigners. I wish you goodnight.'

Having thanked him profusely, I closed the door. The train set off again on its journey and the night steward arrived with a glass of slivovitz and a kind of stale cake which he offered to me to revive my spirits. On leaving the cabin, he said, 'The British have very stubborn natures! God save your Queen!'

I poured the slivovitz down the sink, which probably did wonders for cleaning the train's drains. Then, when I'd cleaned my teeth, I looked at my arms and shoulders, all red and mottled from manhandling. Then I slept. In the morning, I would be in Paris. I wondered if I could get a visa in four hours in order to return to Yugoslavia. If not, how would I get back? I slept, having decided to face all that in the morning. Before I slept, though, I thought of

Mirja, the beautiful Yugoslav actress with whom I'd often talked. She dreamed of going to the States and never returning to Belgrade. Her man friend was a former head of the Secret Police, a very useful man for her to know and so it had proved this night for me, too.

In the morning, I rushed to Repetto, bought my tights and then went to the Yugoslav Embassy for a visa to return. 'It will take forty-eight hours,' they said. When I explained the situation of work, tickets and the impossibility of delaying the return, they replied, 'Forty-eight hours.' I took the train but got off at Trieste, a fascinating city full of strong women and men who pride themselves on their capacity to innovate. I told the raven-haired owner of the restaurant where I ate that I wanted to get back to Belgrade but that I'd 'forgotten' my visa. She arranged everything and, an hour later, I was driven by a man in a very old taxi through beautiful countryside and numerous fields into Yugoslavia. I walked from the arrival point to the village nearby and handed over a note that had been written for me and was taken to the nearest station. I was about to buy a ticket to Belgrade, when a familiar voice said, 'It will be more comfortable in my car.' And it was. The man from the Orient Express drove me back to my hotel. When I asked how he had known I would leave the train in Trieste, he smiled and said, 'In that city everything can be arranged, so I knew you would go there. The rest was easy, very logical, like you.' As I said, a very useful gentleman.

Some years later, I decided to take the Trans-Siberian and immediately received a note from one of my friends:

Darling,

Don't go on the Trans-Siberian. I know you love trains, but it takes so very long and they don't understand things that are important to you, like sleeping in your own cabin and personal hygiene. If you must go, take both berths in a two-berth cabin. And take non-perishable food: tins, salamis, dried figs et cetera, because sometimes the restaurant car disappears. Do tell me what happens on your return.

The note was from a diplomat who had 'done' Russia and was also a great friend. I followed his advice to the letter, unable to imagine that a train journey could be difficult. I spoke ten words of Russian and counted on learning a lot in those long days of the journey. I did.

There was a babushka with a permanently steaming samovar at the end of the carriage. I had taken both berths in the cabin and arrived like a Harrod's food delivery service. First, I strung the salami near the window and then I hid the rest of the food. When everything was arranged to my liking, I sat looking out at the station concourse of Moscow. Peasants wore headscarves and shawls and kept their heads down, as if still expecting the knout. Prostitutes chalked their prices on the soles of their shoes and, when a man passed and enquired they bent one knee, lifted their foot up as far as the bottom and showed him the cost of their services, which saved learning ten foreign languages and all the Russian dialects. Food vendors, illicit money-changers and children offering to carry bags for tips mingled with travellers of every nationality in a curiously colourless kaleidoscope. No one smiled. Few seemed at ease and anyone with charisma was immediately viewed with suspicion, or put under surveillance. No wonder Nureyev fled to the West.

When the train finally took off, I was excited by the idea of the journey and relieved that no one had challenged my single use of a double cabin. I went to make friends with the babushka and drank tea in copious quantities, forgetting its diuretic qualities that became obvious in the middle of the night. Eventually, I went back to my cabin, opened the door and found a large man sitting on my bed.

All Russian passengers don pyjamas shortly after boarding a long distance train and this man was no exception. He had a shock of maize-coloured hair and a vodka-nourished, puce face. He also had a penis reminiscent of Orbiter 1. I saw it forming a kind of ever-pointing signpost to the direction of his thoughts. I told him that this was my cabin. Not understanding a word, he lay down on my bed. I called the train controller who did his best to explain to me that no one slept alone in a cabin for two. I shoved the controller out of the cabin and then tried to throw the elephant man out, too. But he was too heavy for me. Normally I can lift a four-ton lorry if I get angry enough, but I was tired and dispirited as I watched him lying on my bed, looking at my every reaction with his little piggy eyes. I decided that if I couldn't use force to evict him, I had better use guile. But what to do to make him go away? He was obviously not the sensitive type. I decided, after a while, to sing. Louder and louder and out of tune, I sang as if I were going to continue all night. He stuck it out through my rendition of 'Rule Britannia' and 'There'll Always Be an England' and a couple of unsuccessful tries at Bowie's 'Ground Control to Major Tom' lyrics that Paula played five hundred time a day when young. Finally he rose and with a pained expression on his face sauntered back to the corridor and was not seen again for the rest of the journey. I closed the door, locked it and having hit the pillow against the wall a few times in case he had nits, fell asleep until the babushka arrived with tea the following morning.

In the cold light of dawn, I walked up and down the corridor, drinking my tea and taking in the scene. When I returned to my berth, I found a woman going through my bag. I made her leave and then ran after her to check if she'd taken anything. She had. Unhappy that I couldn't leave the cabin without taking everything with me on my back like a snail, I began again to pace up and down the corridor.

It was then that I saw a very old woman, two children and a young woman huddled together on the floor of the wagon along from mine. I asked a young Russian student why they were on the floor and she said they had tickets but not beds. The old woman looked exhausted and the children pale. I went back to my cabin and tried looking at the scenery but I kept thinking of the family with no beds. I told myself that they were used to hard conditions. In Russia at the time, people tolerate medical interventions that would kill most of us. Their clinics were like ours forty years previously. They also survive cold, a poor diet and every form of intense poverty and stress. I told myself I would be unable to sleep if I changed my arrangements. Then I realised that I'd be unable to sleep anyway, if I were selfish enough to keep my cabin all to myself. After a second night of luxurious sleep, I asked the night steward to tell me if I could invite the women and children into my cabin. He said no, under no circumstances. After receiving a generous tip he said he would go and find them immediately.

They stood outside, clutching their one bag. I sat on my bed, wondering what to do to make them at ease without seeming like some capitalist Lady Bountiful. I cut slices of salami and offered them to everyone. I handed them tea, which they looked at but didn't drink, until I began to draw funny animals for the two children. Suddenly, they all laughed and came and sat at my side. Evidently, the way to the Russian heart is via the children. I learned the lesson fast. Then, I removed my things from the lower bed and indicated that they sleep there. The children and I could have the higher bed, to avoid any flying grannies later.

After dinner, I went through my ablutions and got into bed. Too tired to argue, the mother and grandmother slept in one bed, the older child on the floor on an additional mattress and the little one with me. I slept like a log, despite the presence of strangers.

The long journey, some 8,000 kilometres or thereabouts, passed too quickly. The young woman appointed herself my Russian teacher, cabin cleaner and the guardian of my belongings. Granny became tea collector and information gatherer. She and the babushka got on so well that we were spoiled with all manner of treats. As it began to get colder, the children laughed when I slept in my woollen hat and pullover and Scottish golfing socks. Other passengers who had been uncommunicative at the beginning of the journey came and went, bringing sweets for the children and pausing for a word with my companions. A university professor explained in near perfect English where we were, what the flora and fauna of the area was, its history and if it was a 'sensitive' region. The landscape was like a black-and-white film still at certain moments of the day, similar to the north of Scotland when a watery sun touches the larch trees. I never saw the maize-haired man again. My cabin guests ate most of the food and I was delighted to get rid of three of my four stomachs because the lack of exercise made me lose my appetite completely.

The only blot on the copy book of the Trans-Siberian train was a little weasel- like man, who asked me endless questions. I hate questions, but all my life people, some of whom I've never met before and will never meet again, ask me questions. The press ask questions, but rarely print what I say, only what they have been told to believe. If I ever meet an independent-minded journalist capable of telling truth from fiction, I shall marry him! The weasel wanted to know how many languages I spoke, why I was sharing my compartment with so many when I had reserved both berths to be alone. Nowadays, if I meet one of these nosey types, or curiosity-killed-the-cat types, I tell them my life story, but substitute mystery for one of my fictional characters from a past novel. It works very well. I wonder if there are still little weasel men in Russia now after *perestroika*. Or is Russia eternally the same, protected, in Deputy Polivanov's words, by 'impenetrable spaces, impassable mud and the mercy of Saint Nicholas Mirlikisky'. The only thing Russia never managed to protect herself from was the danger within, the power-hungry madmen who scythe down whole generations to gain power and to keep it.

FRIEND OR FOE

I don't know if it is because it was my first experience of life away from England or because it holds so many memories, but Paris has always been high in my affections and it has also been the scene of many interesting moments in my life. It was strange, but perhaps only to be expected that I should be revisited by my past when I was staying there in a fancy hotel near the Place de l'Étoile, many years after I had first arrived to begin my career as a Bluebell.

It was six in the evening when he called.

'After all that's happened to you since we last met, you must be ready to have dinner with me?'

Not recognising the voice, I didn't answer. The caller then gave a very detailed account of my existence since the day when I had left the world of show business to marry Jess. No detail had escaped him; no secret had remained secret. He said finally, 'I'll pick you up at the hotel at seven-thirty. Be ready in the hall.'

I sat for a long time trying to work out how someone could know so much of my life for over a decade. I hadn't been followed. Or had I? Who was he and why had he wanted to know all about me? Half dead with curiosity, I got into the shower, then dressed for dinner and was in the hall of the hotel at seven thirty. I saw a sleek black car pull up and was astounded to see Gianni, the man with the cane from my Lido days. His black hair was now sprinkled with grey, but his unforgettable black eyes were unchanged. Walking towards me, he said, 'I'm so happy to see you again, Helene. I've waited such a long time.'

And suddenly instinct took over, and for once in my life I felt a little bit afraid.

Gianni knew that Paula was in Monaco visiting friends

with Jess and invited me to meet his father. We would travel to Nice in a private plane. I declined. He said, 'I've waited a long time to invite you to dinner please.'

'Just for dinner,' I replied.

When we arrived at our destination, it was immediately obvious that we were not in Nice. Panic hit me when I recognised Palermo.

Sicily is a fascinating island. In the hinterland, there are ancient palaces full of the unique furniture of the region – carved, gilded and embellished with tortoiseshell. The rooms are big and high, furnished with baroque pieces and curtains of heavy velvet, or brocade, in jewel colours, while mirrors reflect crystal chandeliers holding ivory candles of cathedral-like proportions. Here, the men's faces are pale and blue around the chin, even if they shave twice a day. The women wear black in perpetual mourning for men killed in vendettas. Children's games include hanging lizards, shooting rats and, like their fathers, chasing gaily coloured, beautiful butterflies that they put in cages and study from all angles before killing them.

Gianni installed me in an hotel and said he would come for me in the morning and we would have lunch at his home with his father. Then he would take me to meet all his friends. He stressed the 'all' and I wondered what he had in mind, but he left suddenly, a mysterious smile on his face. I couldn't sleep and sat reading in my bed, wondering whether to make a run for it to the airport. Knowing the island and its inhabitants told me that I would never be allowed to take off, because Gianni wouldn't want that. I stayed awake all night and ate breakfast at six. Then I went for a walk in the hotel grounds. A handsome young man followed me at a discreet distance. I began to feel extremely apprehensive and then, suddenly, extremely annoyed. Gianni arrived at ten and drove me to a very beautiful country house about twenty minutes from Palermo.

His father was an elegant, elderly gentleman, only the eyes betrayed a past that was, perhaps, less than gentlemanly. He talked with me and discussed the changes in attitude of Italian film-makers. Gianni scowled and ordered me to accompany him to see the island. 'Ordered' was the word and I didn't like it. Still, I followed him and he showed me the family homes, their land, their mountain, a craggy hill which had a history that seemed to amuse him. Having parked his Ferrari on the edge of the hill, he said, 'Go and look below and you'll understand why we bring our enemies here.'

As I suffer from vertigo, I declined. Gianni's response was a slap on both sides of my face.

'You must learn to be obedient,' he said.

'Dogs are obedient,' I replied. Then I got out of the car, having released the hand brake. While Gianni approached me, with punishment on his mind, the Ferrari slid inexorably forwards and took the same route as his enemies, crashing far below on the rocks. At that moment, I saw his father sitting behind his chauffeur in a very fast

and stylish car. Gianni's screams of rage echoed everywhere. His man ran to the edge of the cliff and looked
down in disbelief. Gianni's father beckoned me and I ran
to his car and was driven away. He was smiling with some
odd, inner pleasure. When he spoke, I smiled, too.

'No one has ever dared disobey Gianni. That's why he
has become so dangerous, even to us. We must get you out
of Sicily immediately.'

I left fifteen minutes later on a fishing boat. My luggage,
small as it was, remained at the hotel. I never saw it again.
Gianni's papa saw me to the boat and explained that there
would be a change of transport 'midway'. I thanked him
for everything and he replied, 'No need for thanks. I wait
thirty years for someone to do that to my son. Try not to
worry Elena. Leave everything to me.'

I returned to Paris, wondering if Gianni was already
after me. He wasn't, but I lived in fear for weeks, until I
received a card on my birthday, a very stylish card of heavy
vellum. Inside was a handwritten message: 'To tell you
Happy Birthday Elena. My son was killed in a car accident
near the cliff a month after your visit. I thought you would
wish to know. Papa.'

I read it and read it again and understood.

CHAPTER SEVENTEEN

A great deal has been written about Hughie Green since his death, most of it offensive. A lot of people have made a lot of money out of him and at least one has 'bent' the law for gain.

I met Hughie at the hotel in Wales, very briefly the first time, as he was running to his car after lunching in the dining room. Jess called me and said, 'Come and meet Hughie Green. Hurry! He's on stage at two-thirty.'

I had never heard of Hughie and was a bit surprised that Jess was so anxious for him to stay in the hotel. It was part of his search for celebrities who would be willing to give the place a bit of free publicity. That first time, I found Hughie well mannered and elegant, but given to pulling weird faces every few seconds.

His second visit, at the end of summer, was a short stay. He came with a very beautiful blonde girl and they invited Jess and me to have coffee with them in the Welsh Kitchen bar on the night of their departure. On reaching the front door of the hotel, en route to Hughie's car, they shook hands and said goodbye. Then the young lady asked Jess if she could kiss me. 'Of course dear,' said Jess in his best paternal voice. She kissed me full on the mouth, pinning me to the wall for what seemed like an age! Jess' mouth dropped open and as they walked to their car, he said, 'I hope she doesn't come again! If my mother had seen that, she would have thought it very odd. She would have asked questions.'

Hughie came again another time for afternoon tea, with another beautiful girl, who proceeded to fellate him with enthusiasm, just as the waiters were entering with their trays. Cups rattled, but the young men managed to avoid dropping the lot on the floor. I don't recall any other visits, though there were four bars in the hotel and he could have visited one of those, but I have no recollection of seeing him around the hotel again.

Years later, though, we met again in London. Hughie took me to dinner and then back to his apartment. I had always felt curious about him, so the outcome was predictable. In writing this, I have rarely felt as confused as when I tried to analyse what went wrong that first time with Hughie. For him, making love was a routine, his version of the American 'wham, bam and thank you ma'am'. That's fine by me, no problem. The fault of the failure was with me.

First, I felt traumatised by the apartment's atmosphere. Since childhood, I have been hyper-sensitive to the 'feel' of people and places. I kept asking myself what manner of man could live in such a world of ghostly grey emptiness and that made me revise my idea of Hughie. Second, for reasons I can't remember now, once we began to make love, I thought of my mother-in-law, Sybil, who, before becoming an accomplished painter of seascapes had gently entered the magic world of art via painting by numbers. Hughie made love with efficiency. I found his pale body attractive, but his technique was a variation on the theme of painting by numbers – fornication by numbers.

The next time we were intimate, after Hughie flew me to Manchester to open a bowling alley, it happened in the warm cosiness of a grand hotel. I felt more involved that time, despite the 'by numbers' technique. It was a pleasant evening full of laughter but I don't recall that we ever made love again, as I left England shortly afterwards.

Looking back, I remember best being with Hughie and his friends. I liked them all, especially Mr and Mrs Sharples. Hughie functioned very little on an emotional level, except when it came to his work. His work was his life and he never changed. His friends were almost all connected with his work. It was his world.

I like remembering my terror on thinking of being

flown to a professional engagement in Manchester by Hughie, who offered to take me because a train strike would have prevented me from getting there. I was terrified, thinking Hughie the joker flying a plane. I didn't know anything about his past in the Royal Canadian Air Force and wondered if he was having me on. From the moment I stepped inside the plane with a couple of his friends, I saw an astonishing metamorphosis. Hughie put on the headphones and began talking to air traffic control. His face was stern, his concentration total. I was amazed but reassured.

Much later, when I was in Palma, I received a call from a *News of the World* writer. He asked me if I knew that my ex-husband was a paedophile. I was very rude and put the phone down. Then I rang Jess to warn him. As Jess' only interest in life was large breasts and there aren't any children with 40-inch chest measurements, I was unworried. Jess, however, panicked and invited his sixteen-year-old girlfriend on holiday to prove his 'normality'. He was immediately sacked by YTV.

When I was told that he and Hughie were enemies, I couldn't believe it. I prefer to remember them laughing together like two mischievous boys, not two ageing men squabbling over a pretty girl. I never believed that their dispute was professional.

When I attended Paula's funeral in the autumn of 2000, I was approached by an elegant blonde person who said she was Hughie's daughter. We talked amicably and I expressed surprise that the *News of the World* journalist had written an article on Hughie being Paula's father. Hughie's daughter said, 'You must have told my father he was Paula's father or he wouldn't have known.'

'I never discussed this subject with Hughie,' I replied.

'Well, only you could have known,' she said.

'As my husband and I were rarely out of bed in the first six months of the marriage, breaking two beds in less than two months, why on earth would I have imagined such a story?' I replied.

Later on, when Christopher Green, Hughie's son, wrote a book about his father with the aid of a professional writer, he explained the situation in his own erroneous fashion: 'Helene knew that Hughie was the father because the year they were married Jess was ill and they hardly ever made love.'

Oh no, Christopher! You and your ghostwriter believed what the newspaper cuttings said, based on yet another of Paula's lies, that she was born in 1960. She wasn't. Paula was conceived in 1958, when Jess was on top form. She was born in 1959 and was three months old when Jess became ill and we temporarily stopped making love. That was the year when the 'unknown man' entered our bedroom and I thought he was there to steal my child. But people believe what they want to believe. When the story came out, there were, inevitably, loads of trashy comments. One journalist commented that Paula had a long chin just like Hughie's, but my grandmother had a long chin, so what did that prove? And to my mind, Paula was Jess personified in almost all of her habits.

I do know that some years before, according to Hughie's friend, Mrs Sharples, Hughie had commented on hearing that Paula was born in 1960, 'Oh, I could have been her father' and that some rumours circulated that it was Hughie who found Paula a job in television, when in fact it was the late Peter Jackson, then editor of the *Television Times*. And a journalist friend also told me that Hughie Green had refused to let the story of Paula's paternity be published, saying, 'Helene will deny it.'

Well, of course, I would have denied it, because I have no recollection of our having made love until after my separation from Jess. But the problem is, one can't help wondering, and I particularly wonder why neither Jess nor Hughie said anything when they were alive. After the incidents that I remember at the hotel, when I realised that Jess had been drugging my hot chocolate, I did become very suspicious of what might have happened and I now believe that anything could have been possible. Of course if Jess and Hughie had said anything, they would also have had to do a lot of explaining.

The awful thing is that the story broke only when everyone concerned, except Paula and I, was dead and I believe that the shock of the article hastened Paula's decline.

I've thought a great deal about it all and I remembered one day that in Sicily mothers teach their children to search for the person who really profits from betrayal. I know who benefited from the betrayal of Paula. There are quite a few and some pretended to be her friends.

Hughie was surely more complex than I realised, but I really knew him only briefly. His friends and those who worked with him liked him and admired his professionalism. As for me, I remember him as the pilot, talking to the control tower. I like to think that that was the real Hughie Green.

PART FOUR

THE GIRL WITH BLUE GLASS EYES

Tread lightly, she is near
Under the snow,
Speak gently, she can hear
The daisies grow.

OSCAR WILDE, 1854-1900, 'REQUIESCAT'

CHAPTER EIGHTEEN

My daughter had various nicknames when small. Little Miss Horridstench was the first, related to the contents of her nappy. Then, in quick succession: Fairy Roundbum, Miss Bossyboots, Paula the Pixie and Princess Paula. She liked the latter so much that for a good eight or nine years she remained Princess Paula. From her earliest days, she wanted to be famous and did everything she could to be noticed to the point where it became a bit worrying, but we all decided it was part of her character and we should accept it. We didn't see the danger for her, or for us, of this obsession. We should have.

There were no problems in the first eleven months of her life apart from the usual teething and crying pitifully if left alone, even for a few minutes. One day, to try to cure this,

I put the television on and found only the test card and music. Paula jogged up and down in her cot to the drumbeats and never cried again. Even as a baby she liked noise, music and people around. The only thing I couldn't solve was her habit of calling me Dadamama. I felt like an African tribal chief once she began to talk and shouted 'Dadamama! Dadamama!' fifty times a day. Jess didn't have a name and neither did anyone else, until she was more than a year old, though she adored it when he put her in her carrying cot, plonked it by the side of the piano and played his favourite tunes, singing like Gracie Fields or Maria Callas, depending on his mood.

When Paula was eleven months old, we all went to Paris on the plane from Manchester. She sat calmly on my knee and we had a lovely time , except that Jess had a panic attack while driving round the Arc de Triomphe. He stopped the car and leaped out, leaving me with Paula on my knee wondering what to do. Finally, I put Paula on my coat on the floor in front of the passenger seat and took over at the wheel. Oblivious to the tooting of horns and shrieking drivers, I sounded my horn as loudly as everyone else and manoeuvred my way towards the Avenue Wagram. Jess avoided us for a few hours, but eventually turned up at the hotel. On our return, we were photographed at the airport by a newsman. It was Paula's first public appearance and she brought it off much better than I did.

A month later, she developed rubella (German measles)

and was really ill. Jess and I were shattered when, on recovering, she refused to eat. The only thing I could get her to accept were chocolate, milk and occasionally an egg or some boiled potatoes. This diet continued until she was eight, until after the most serious of all her illnesses – an atypical pneumonia later called legionnaires' disease but not discovered at the time – when she weighed no more than a four-year-old. When she recovered, she began to eat proper meals four or five times a day and did this for the next eight years.

Our favourite game during Paula's early years was throwing stones into the sea and making them bounce. The Conway Estuary in all its beauty was at the bottom of the garden, so it was wonderful on summer afternoons. In winter, when it rained and was cold, we liked searching for 'treasure' in trunks in the playroom. There, Paula found her favourite toy, my old teddy bear, Bruin, and her other most desired object, my black wig. When she wanted to hide, she put this on and believed implicitly that no one knew her.

She also had a curious habit of always wanting a hat on her head, probably because for years she had very little hair. She appeared at various times in Jess' Austrian felt with a feather, my Durex diaphragm and her plastic potty. She also loved hiding and often stuck her head behind the nearest curtain, thinking no one could see her because she couldn't see them. She never realised that she'd left her bottom outside the curtain, beside Snowy, the cat, who was a bodyguard of superhuman dimensions and totally devoted to her.

During the years at the hotel, Paula was almost always with me. At one time, when the work in the hotel became burdensome and exhausting, I took on a nanny for her. Then, shortly after her arrival, I heard the nanny saying, 'No, you can't go to see your mummy and if you do that again, I shall never let you see your mummy again.' Paula screamed, as if stabbed. I had survived all Gertrude's threats during my childhood, but I still remember them and my terror when she threatened to put me in the orphanage if I disobeyed. I didn't need a threatening nanny for my child and sent the girl packing on the next train. After that we didn't have any nannies, just Snowy the cat, who went everywhere with Paula and me and growled like a dog if anyone approached.

When I went away for the day, Paula either went to my brother- and sister-in-law's which she enjoyed because they had no children and when their hotel was closed for the winter, she had their 'undivided attention'. She also stayed with them for weekends, particularly when I was in Rome for those three months working on Fellini's film. Paula called them 'aquarium weekends' because Teddy and Joey had an aquarium in the hotel which they all adored. Alternatively, she stayed at home with her gran and Jess and went to the village school. Rome had been my one long absence from my child. When I returned, I told Paula that as I was going to be a writer I would not need to go away again, and I didn't.

In fact, I was only ever away for short periods, such as when Jess sent me to audition girls for his summer season show in one of the bars, or for the so-called pin-up photo sessions that later caused such problems with my mother and then with me. Still, Paula didn't like me out of her sight and I once found her hiding behind the curtains in the office where I'd gone to discuss menus with the chef. When I saw Paula's feet sticking out from under the curtains, I took her on my knee and she sat silent and content that I'd let her have her way.

Teddy once said, 'You should have christened that child Glue!' and even Paula in her writing admitted being a clinging vine, sticking close to me morning, noon and night in an obsessional fashion. Why she did this, who knows? Our 'togetherness' augmented once we went to live in Plas Yn Roe. Jess was often absent at auctions or because of work and Paula was happy to have me to herself. I was hers and she made it clear in no uncertain way, young as she was. Paula loved the house in Roewen, the surrounding woods that were full of animals, our routines, such as a morning walk with the cats, and our laughter when I, who detest snow, had to clear two tracks each morning in order to drive the car down or to let the milk and post van deliveries arrive and leave. But what Paula liked best was the Christmas tree field and my perpetual battle with the brambles, which she commentated on as if it were an outside broadcast.

The first serious problem arose when she had to go to

school. Paula hated this and was bitterly resentful that I sent her. The village school was at the bottom of our drive and I walked her there in the morning and back later in the afternoon. She had never been able to stand it if I was out of her sight. The happy situation that had existed when we first arrived at the house changed, because even at weekends when there was no school, Paula screamed and cried if she couldn't see her mum.

I remember once, when she was ill with yet another chest infection, the family doctor said, 'She must drink more, Elaine, or the medication won't circulate.' I replied that she hated water and when ill wouldn't even drink milk or tea. The only things she wanted were Coca-Cola or another fizzy drink like orangeade or raspberryade.. 'Then go to the village and buy a supply,' he replied.

I went to tell my mother-in-law what the doctor had said and asked her to come and stay with Paula while I went to the village. Sybil sat next to her bed while I explained, 'I'm going to the village to buy pop for you. I'll be back in fifteen minutes.'

When I returned, I found Sybil distraught and furious and Paula purple in the face and screaming hysterically. 'What happened?' I asked.

Sybil replied in a tight little voice, 'The moment you went out, she started howling, "Mummy has left me to go to the village." I explained that she had to drink to make her medicine work and as she wouldn't drink you'd gone to buy what she likes. She ignored what I said and just screamed and screamed. You'll have to ask the doctor about these attacks she has every time you go out, even to clear snow! It's not normal.'

Was it to get attention? I've often wondered. Or was it the first sign of worse to come?

CHAPTER NINETEEN

A year and a half after starting school, Paula could still not read or write. I was called in to see the head-mistress, who informed me that if my child continued to be incapable or unwilling to learn to read and write, she would be classified as educationally sub-normal. I returned home furious at her comments, perfectly well aware that Paula was not sub-normal but conscious of the fact that she hated school and was capable of doing anything to escape it. We were lucky that I had just read of an American system used to help dyslexic children learn to read and write. Big cards, about a foot square were cut out and then each letter of the alphabet traced with thick red lines to stand out from the background. I suggested to Paula that we make some such cards at home and we set to work immediately on the project. Paula knew almost the entire alphabet four days later by the time we'd finished crayoning in the red letters. From time to time, I pretended to have forgotten a letter and she loved 'helping' me to remember. It took three weeks for her to learn to write simple words and read captions.

I think Paula just preferred being at home to going to school, even though she made friends. I well remember a beautiful little girl, called Linda Doylerush and the Hughes twins (both boys) from the farm next door, who often came to play and eat beans on toast or a slice of my famous cake that Paula called 'bungo' because it was so heavy. They didn't care, though; they were too busy laughing. I just wanted Paula to be happy and I often let her stay with me if she was a bit under the weather. Once she had learned to read she did well at school, but the incident had made me doubt the educational system. How many timid or bored pupils are classified as educationally sub-normal when they aren't? My child never looked back, thanks to that magazine article that explained how to teach your child to read when the school could not.

The first jarring incident in what seemed to be an ideal mother-child relationship was when I heard an animal screaming in pain and knew it was Snowy, Paula's guardian cat. Looking out of the window, I saw her trying to pull off Snowy's front legs by tearing them apart from his body. Her face was pale, her eyes unblinking. Horrified, I rushed outside and pulled her hands off the cat and said, 'Why did you do that? Snowy's been your friend since you were born. You must never hurt a little animal who loves you.'

No reaction.

A zombie, staring into space.

Chilled, I said, 'Come into the house and we'll have our elevenses,' and I turned to walk away.

Seconds later, Snowy started screaming again. Paula was repeating what she had done. This time I ran outside, liberated Snowy and gave Paula the only smacked bottom she ever had in her young life. Then I went to my room and cried and cried, sure that I was a failure as a mother and unable to comprehend my strange, catatonic child. I had given Paula love and taught love. But she had always liked turning on people she loved. What did it all mean?

When I went downstairs, she was still sitting in the hall, staring out of the window with her blue glass eyes. Then, suddenly, she rose and said, 'I hope you've made biscuits, those that are gooey in the middle, because you've not cooked them enough. I love those, Mummy. I could eat at least twenty.'

For a while after this incident, Paula returned to normal. She was home loving and rather lazy, but given to lapses of concentration when she appeared to lose the real world. During these periods, if I talked to her, she seemed unaware of my words until reality returned. She was very proud of having a young mother and a beautiful one. At the same time, she suffered from jealousy and no amount of reassurance that she too would be beautiful worked. She was the only small child I ever met who wanted to be 6 feet tall with long red hair. Failing that, she did everything she could to be noticed and she had all our attention. Since we had been told when Paula was most ill that she might not live until ten years old, we'd spoilt her to death. I spoilt her more than everyone else put together and I certainly paid for it later, but at the time it seemed the thing to do. I loved her so much.

A much more serious event came a month later. Paula was one her way to the front door when someone knocked. On my way downstairs, I said, 'Open the door, please, and say I'm on my way.' I was horrified to hear Paula say in a strangely disembodied but venomous voice, 'My mummy hates you.'

My best woman friend, shattered by this greeting, burst into tears and ran to her car. She never came back and never believed that I had not said it. It was a sad day for me, because it was evident that Paula had discovered the power of the lie and there was the even more dangerous realisation that she had been believed when I had not. Power corrupts and the power of the lie corrupted my child.

I asked her, 'Why did you do that?' She did not reply. Instead, predictably, those blue glass eyes of hers stared out across the valley and she became unreachable.

I called the doctor, who came in his reassuring tweed suit, listened solemnly to the story and then asked, 'Does she often stare like this?'

'She's done it four or five times before.'

He led me out of the room and watched as I made tea and cut slices of my heavy 'bungo' fruit cake that he too adored.

'Paula's out of balance because of pathological jealousy and it will get worse as she grows up, Elaine. More worrying is that she may be showing signs of a serious condition. If anything like this happens again, she must see a psychiatrist.'

All this happened just over forty years ago, when we none of us knew a great deal about psychiatry and its advantages. I didn't even know that pathological liars existed and had never heard of certain perversions. Looking back, I can't believe I was as green as I was, but it was like that. My reaction to the doctor's words was to feel insulted on Paula's behalf. I didn't know what to say and so said very little. Then, when he had gone, I telephoned my friend and was anguished when she refused to discuss the incident and told me never to call again. Her words remained with me for ever, 'Why,' she asked, 'would an innocent little girl like Paula lie?'

Why indeed? It was a question I was to ask myself very often over the next thirty years of being lied about by the daughter I loved.

All the days were not like that one, some were totally hilarious, like when Paula asked about babies. 'I know mummies keep them in their stomach while they grow, but how do they get there?' Sex is always good for a laugh. Tell a child the facts of life in a direct way and with ordinary words and the odds are she'll howl with laughter and cry out frequently, for weeks on end at the most inopportune moment, 'Did my granny do that?' 'Did the headmistress to it?' 'Did the vicar do it?' Worse, at some public function of incredible pomposity, 'Did that man with the chain round his shoulders do it, Mummy?' All this accompanied by more howls of laughter, hers and mine, at the sheer lunacy of the human reproductive process. Paula was no exception and I thought she would never stop asking embarrassing questions about the most conventional of our friends. Once, in Spain, we were invited by a lady with eleven children to visit. Her husband was a desiccated looking weakling and I said to Paula, 'Please don't make me laugh!'

She looked at me out of the corner of her eye and said, 'He did it too much, didn't he, Mummy?'

Then she watched his every move, as if observing a rare animal. The Spaniard was flattered and smiled showing a mouthful of yellow teeth. His wife snapped at Paula to go and play in the garden. I had a better idea. I took her home.

CHAPTER TWENTY

One autumn, when Paula was about fourteen, I proposed that she should accompany me to New York, where I was going to see my American agent and publishers. Paula was euphoric, sure that instant fame awaited her the moment she stepped off the plane. The reality was less acceptable. At Kennedy Airport, the luggage from our flight took four hours to appear and I, exhausted by the journey and pale with annoyance, decided that I would never travel anywhere, no matter for how long, with more than a shoulder bag and I haven't changed my mind. Thirty-odd years have gone by and I still travel with a marvellous shoulder bag that I bought in London's South Molton Street. Paula viewed my decision with her usual glorious mum-mockery.

'You'll be able to put the essentials in a shoulder bag, Mummy, a two-gallon bottle of scent and a spare pair of stiletto heels.'

We stayed in a hotel that no longer exists, built directly over the concourse of Grand Central Station. As I love trains, it was fine, but the windows were sealed and an autumn heat wave vied with the pre-programmed central heating to turn both of us puce. I plead the Fifth Amendment as to the broken window in our bedroom that restored normal breathing. Unsurprised by my actions, Paula wrote to her granny saying, 'Mummy has chosen our hotel because the railroad runs through the middle of the house.'

We visited the Guggenheim, the Met, Central Park and Macy's where we bought Paula a Snoopy bed quilt. She liked everything that small children like. My friend Amelia once said, 'How old is your daughter, eight or nine?' When I said thirteen, she couldn't believe it. In New York, however, Paula strived to be sophisticated and was thrilled when I let her come with me in response to a dinner invitation by one of my editors, her husband and parents. We had dinner in Chinatown. Everything was delicious and the company was elegant. We were being driven home afterwards when, on stopping at a red light, a gang fight broke out. One of the gang members, wanting to stay safe behind the cover of the car, lay down with his head under the front wheel, so we were stuck. Then bullets began to whistle past and I called to the driver, who seemed momentarily paralysed, 'Drive on, accelerate!'

'He has his head under my front wheel,' replied the elegant young man.

Paula grasped my hand, as the noise of conflict continued.

'Drive on, or we'll all be killed,' I said, and with great courage he did just that. The head with the body attached disappeared to a side street and the battle resumed in the black murk of a New York alley. 'You were just like Clint Eastwood, Mummy,' Paula whispered. I wasn't sure if it was a compliment, but it didn't matter. We were both very happy to arrive at our old-fashioned hotel and retire to the peace of our room.

Of that trip, two things remain in my memory. The first is the day when Paula saw a major book promotion in a 5th Avenue store for a biography called *Mummy Dearest* and read in the write-ups that Joan Crawford's adopted daughter had made a million from the book, become famous overnight and had seriously upset her mother's reputation to the point of ruining her. For the rest of the trip, Paula read the cuttings and dreamed. The other memory is of my purchase of a truly wondrous kaleidoscope. There were no little pieces as there are in old-fashioned kaleidoscopes. This one used existing light and the viewer's surroundings to form marvellous, Vasarely-like images in colours related to the room, or the location of the viewing. We were in the plane coming home when Paula discovered that the kaleidoscope was made in France.

'Oh Mummy, you have very French taste, even when you shop in New York.'

'Snoopy bedcovers aren't French.'

'Patou perfume is.'

During our visit that year, we had discovered a perfect beach on Long Island, devoid of all commerce, just sea, sky and an endless ribbon of golden sand. In the distance, a line of Gatsby mansions, built in the thirties, stood sentinel on this wonderful place. Paula thought it fine 'for five minutes'.

'The only thing it lacks is people, Mummy. There's no noise, no music, no crowd.'

I marvelled at how different we could be in many ways, yet our lives had both seen their fair share of problems. We didn't really argue, but we were at opposite ends of every spectrum in life. I considered my teenage daughter to be a very modern party person in embryo. She considered me to be a glamorous lady with the mind of a medieval monk and some very eccentric ideas. The differences made us both laugh when she was young, which is how it should be. On our return, Paula related her favourite moments on the phone to Sybil.

'What I liked were the hamburgers and that Greek restaurant where the owner shouted, "Lunch for a child" for Mummy, because she can't eat those big American platefuls. And I liked the fortune cookie with my Chinese meal, because it said I should wear a tiara someday. Perhaps I'll marry a prince.'

My mother always wanted me to marry a prince and was seriously disappointed when I remained a mere mortal, due to a nature that shuns *la vie sociale* and a galloping fear of formality. Paula's stardust ideas were like listening to Gertrude's dreams, or Jess' longing to be Al Capone or Liberace.

Many years later, Paula posed for *Tatler* in a tiara and I felt the dawning of terror that she had crossed the line between reality and fiction and no longer knew the difference. The febrile look in her eyes on that photo chilled me for weeks.

CHAPTER TWENTY-ONE

I had liked the idea of living abroad in the sunshine and far from Jess, but where to live was governed by the presence or absence of a good English school. On our first visit to the island of Majorca in 1971, we had checked out a school for Paula. We liked it and now needed a house for the future. We were both very excited at the prospect of a new life, a new beginning. I went to see an estate agent to ask him to find me a property, not more than five miles from Palma and within a certain price range. I was due to receive a cheque and hoped to use part of it to finance the purchase. I was lucky that Majorca had not yet attracted the so-called beautiful people. At that time it was often derided as being vulgar and full of fat beer bellies turning day-glo puce in the sun at Arenal. I had learned from my childhood in Blackpool that beaches attract crowds and had always sought silence and peace. In the seventies, you didn't have to go far in Majorca to find your own 'Innisfree' and the tranquillity of the bee-loud glade.

The agent was young, elegant and came from a good family. He told me immediately that what I wanted was impossible to find so near the city of Palma. He showed me many beautiful houses further away and one or two of those ancient Spanish town houses with hidden courtyards. I adore secret places and would dearly have loved to but a townhouse, but they cost five times as much as I could have hoped to pay.

After endless days of frustration, we went off to search for what Paula and I called 'our house'. It was the agent's week away in Barcelona and we felt a bit awed by the idea of trying to find a property alone. On the road from Palma to Valdemossa, Paula complained of feeling car-sick. Like my mother-in-law, she was very sensitive to certain kinds of movement. I was debating whether to turn back and return to the hotel in Palma, when we were stopped by Spanish traffic police and hauled out of the car, without any pretence of politeness. Paula immediately vomited over one of the policeman's boots. Then we were waved on in a manner usually reserved for criminals and hit-and-run drivers, not sedately driving mothers with thirteen-year-old daughters aboard. I was so angry at their attitude and the fact that they had upset my child, I drove off the main road on to a small track, which led through pink-flowering fruit orchards to a nearby white village. Having parked the car, I led Paula to the village bar and ordered tea for her and an *ensaimada*, a round, sugary pastry that she adored. I drank a gallon of mineral water and two black coffees and told the bar owner and his wife about the two traffic policemen. When I said Paula had been so upset that she had vomited, the owner spat on the floor and said some very rude, but deliciously funny, things about the patrolmen's mothers, grandmothers and ancestors in general.

I asked his wife if there were any houses for sale in the village and she told me that one had just come on the market. It was a good solid house but had no electricity, or mains drainage, or running water. The bar owner's mother led us to the house, a long *finca*, narrow from front to back, with a vine-laden trellis that shaded the front terrace. It had a well, an exterior bread oven and, most important of all, a rectangular garden with a pomegranate, a kaki and two almond trees. I loved it at once and so did Paula.

We were told the price by one of the neighbours, who was also one of the heirs named in the former owner's will. Ten days later, I bought the house. Paula and I watched, wide eyed, as nine heirs, all dressed in black, signed the sale agreement, solemn faced, with a thumb print because none of them could read or write. It was the first time I realised the difference, in the Spain of General Franco, between the government and professional classes and those who dwelt in the countryside. Educated Spain had great style; rural Spain was real.

Before finally departing England for Majorca, I asked Jess to sign a covenant leaving the part of the house he would inherit from his mother to Paula and my part was assigned to him on this condition. If, for any reason this was not left to Paula, I was to be paid half the value of the house at the time of Jess' death. The covenant was signed in the offices of Gamlin, Kelly & Beatty in Rhyl. A few years later, at the time of the Jess–Anita Kay scandal, I contacted these solicitors and asked for a copy of the covenant. I received a reply telling me that it could not be found. Neither could the two ladies who had witnessed it. The partner who had drafted it was no longer alive. I was mystified, and remain so.

Paula and I travelled to Majorca via Southampton, Bilbao and Barcelona. The crossing was very rough and I succeeded in being sick for the entire thirty-seven hours. Then Paula accidentally trapped the cabin stewardess' head in the door when she was bringing me some medication. We were both glad to disembark and drive away in our funny Fiat van full of our possessions.

The AA had warned me that petrol pumps were hard to find between Bilbao and Vittoria, where I planned to stay the night, so I asked Paula to keep an eye open for one. She variously pointed out advertising signs for the El Corte Inglés chain of department stores, bullfights and sangria, but no petrol stations. We arrived safely at our hotel, however, ate a huge dinner and slept at once. The following morning, I drove us to Barcelona, where, at the port, they told me that as it was the Easter fiesta, so there would be no sailings to Palma for two days. I consulted my *Hotels of Europe* book and drove off to find us somewhere to say.

The chosen hotel had twenty-four-hour-a-day security in the garage for our van. I drove around for ages trying to find it, until, tired and anxious, I had to stop to rest. It was then that Paula said, 'Look Mummy, that's our hotel!' I'd pulled up just outside it.

On our arrival in Palma, we went to the bank. Weeks before, I had arranged for one of the cheques to be sent directly there. It had not arrived. This left me with £20 in cash. Paula stared into space, unable to work out what to do. I filled the van with petrol and bought a large bottle of perfume to cheer myself up. Better to have nothing than a tenner to last for ever!

We then drove to the farmhouse, expecting to find it habitable. I was shocked to see that in the months since our last visit nothing at all had been done. I unloaded the van and drove back to the builder's office in Palma, where I did a good imitation of the Terminator. The builder was tiny and obviously shocked. At one point, he jumped on a chair so he could appear bigger than me and said, 'We shall all be there in the morning, señora.' And they were.

By early evening, Paula and I were famished, so I took her to a local bistro where we had often eaten before and said to the owner that I would like to eat each day with my child, but that I couldn't pay until our cheque arrived from

America. Then I consulted a menu, ordered and began to chat to a very wide-eyed Paula. The owner opened his mouth, then shut it again. Then he went into the kitchen, returning some time later with two enormous plates of food. We ate there twice a day for two more weeks until, finally the money arrived. I paid in full and we continued as customers until we left Majorca.

One day, when he knew me better, the owner said, 'My wife nearly kill me when I accept, but I knew you were an English gentleman and they always pay'. It was the only time in my life that anyone called me a gentleman.

Three weeks after our arrival, a very old lady appeared. I served her coffee and chocolate tart on the terrace. After her second slice of tart, the old lady said, 'Señora, if you would like some furniture, I will give you all I have in the garage of my house and also two of the beds from inside. I do so want some of those white beds they are selling in the new galleries in Palma, but the old furniture takes all the spare space.'

A new department store had opened recently in Palma, selling all-white, painted furniture which, to my astonishment, was greatly sought after by the locals. The real surprise for me came, however, when I saw the furniture the old woman had relegated to the garage – an ancient, upright sofa of pale oak with a rattan seat, a traditional single bed with barley-twirled posts, a writing desk with drawers on either side of a central aperture and the two beds she wished removed from the house, both of which were made of carved wood and were solid and ancient. Realising that without any effort on my part, I had acquired the basic furniture of the entire house, free, I was overcome with gratitude.

The old lady said, 'It's nothing, señora. I am grateful to you, because now I can have lots of white furniture.'

Later, I went out and bought mattresses for the beds, a fridge, a cooker and a couple of modern sofas that could be used as divans. The local men acquired hernias carrying boxes of books into the house for us and two new women friends planted the little garden that edged the vine terrace.

Paula and I were as happy as kings.

Suddenly 'home' was emerging and with it hopes for a sun-filled future. When work resumed, we discovered with something of a shock that the house had new plumbing, a bath, toilets and shiny porcelain sinks, but no cesspit. Digging began. The neighbours watched from the end of the garden, as if life were a circus. One showed me how to eat the fruit off the kaki tree. I turned out to be a poor pupil and had a prune-wrinkled mouth for days. I gave all the kaki fruit to my neighbours after this experience and showed them the inside of my mouth by way of explaining my rejection of the fruit. I never ate kaki again and Paula didn't even try.

'It's not *English* fruit, Mummy.'

I tried for eighteen years to get her to view foreign places as 'different' – England as English, Spain as Spanish, Italy as Italian and so on, but she remained resolutely provincial, viewing all food with a foreign name as deeply suspicious, foreign languages as impossible and undesirable, rejecting everything foreign except for the sun and swimming.

Before that summer, Palma suffered such rainstorms as had not been seen for thirty years. The potato crops rotted in the ground and leaden skies prevented folk from venturing outside for long. I drove Paula to school each morning and then went back home to work. I returned to the school in the afternoon and brought her back to the house. Normally, we went first to the beach to eat when she left school. On rainy days, we went home and baked cakes. Then Paula broke the world-eating record and ate the lot. Now a teenager, she had thrown out all her fine clothes in favour of faded jeans and diverse dirty t-shirts.

One day, as I neared the house, I found the drive blocked by an ancient car belonging to one of the heirs who had sold the property to me and who had come some weeks previously with the intention of exercising his dog in my garden. Leaving Paula in the van, I walked through the downpour to his house, which was close by, to ask him to let me pass. Seeing me soaked to the skin, he smiled in triumph. I said nothing. What can one say to a man like that? The next day, as it rained yet again, his car blocked the drive again and he was not at home. I had to leave the van on the road and carry my daughter to the house. I was terrified in case she got soaked to the skin and became ill again. We had had enough of illness. The man's wife was embarrassed, but didn't know where he was. I said, as I passed on foot along the drive, 'I hope he stops playing games soon.'

She was a very kind woman, and I couldn't understand why she put up with her husband's odd behaviour. His greatest neighbourly accomplishment was to run over as many of the local cats as possible, so I was in no mind to put up with this man any longer. It continued to rain night and day and this neighbour continued his one-upmanship game. Then, during the worst storm ever, his car blocked my entry again. The man stood on his terrace smoking a cow-dung cigarette and smiling triumphantly. I got out of my van and went to ask if he would move his car. He didn't reply, just looked at me with defiance and flicked a load of cigarette ash in my direction. He was proving to me that he controlled my life.

I spoke very quietly, 'Señor Chavez, please move your car.'

No reply.

'If you don't move it, I shall ram it.'

His laughter came from somewhere deep within. Realising that he knew little of the British character, I returned to the van, reversed to give me a good run up and rammed his boneshaker which skidded away and fell on its side.

Paula was enrolled in the English School, where she objected to having to learn Spanish. One day she said to me, 'Why can't they speak English?' and I replied, 'In Spain, they speak Spanish; in France, French; in Portugal,

Portuguese and when we live in their country, we have to learn their language, or we can't make friends and cope with emergencies. If they come to England to live, they have to learn English.'

Paula scowled and said, 'Mummy, I refuse to learn Spanish.' And I don't think she ever did.

She made friends at school with a very nice young girl, Gayle Coull, who lived in the next apartment to ours once I sold the farmhouse to move nearer to Paula's school. Gayle's mother, Lilian, was a very interesting lady – elegant, full of fun and with impeccable manners, like her daughter. Gayle came on holiday with us to Marbella and was the only person Paula missed when we left Majorca. I was very touched when she wrote to me after Paula's death. She continues the contact and I hope to see her again someday.

It was in Majorca that Paula became a typical teenager. Generally there were few problems, apart from one or two very unsuitable boys who pursued her. One of them, who was twice her age, I had to see on to the boat to Ibiza to get rid of him. Paula finally settled her sights on a Spanish teenager, who came to the house. He was handsome, charming and fun. Paula was a woman in many respects now, but still essentially a child and she remained a child to the end of her life. Some people do.

When the headmaster of the school retired, Paula had just taken her O Levels and, given that the brilliant Oxford double first was to be replaced by a kind and gentle lady with only primary-school qualifications, I decided that Paula needed a firm hand and probably additional tuition if she were to get any A Levels. I therefore sent her to my old school, Elmslie, for three terms and while she was there she lived *en famille* with my Aunt Marjorie, who was herself an affectionate and concerned mother of two girls.

Unfortunately, Paula hated Elmslie, England, school generally and became seriously angry. I returned to England, where I had bought a holiday house in Sussex with my earnings from my writing and some of the proceeds from the sale of my apartment in Majorca. Paula went from Elmslie to a sixth-form college in Oxford at the suggestion of her godfather. She came home most weekends and eventually gained two A Levels, which made me very proud.

I suggested lunch to celebrate at Fortnum's Fountain Room, our favourite eating place since Paula was 3½. On the day, I took the train to London and waited under Fortnum's clock, as I always had in the past.

Paula stepped out of a taxi, dressed as I had never seen her. She was wearing filthy, white rubber, knee-length trousers under a white tutu-style skirt held up with pins. She looked awful and her hair was as dirty as the rest of her. It was another stage of her transformation. The next time I saw her, she was talking with a south London accent.

This time I ignored the dirt, gave her a big kiss and said, 'Shall we go in? I'm so hungry.'

Paula stopped, stared and then, visibly annoyed, said,

'Are you taking me in dressed like this, Mummy?'

'Of course, that's why we came isn't it?'

Lunch was tense. For the first time Paula was ill at ease in the Fountain Room. I don't know what reaction she had expected, or wanted, but my own lack of disapproval displeased her. She sulked through lunch, ate, but barely spoke and I returned home thinking that after fourteen years of regular visits, the Fountain Room was finished, at least for me. Later, Paula took a journalist friend there often, so what had obviously displeased her was not the place, but me. She had wanted to provoke me into telling her off, but she should have known that for all my faults, I don't condemn what is different, especially teenagers who are finding their style.

The most memorable moment of the following year was a phone call from Paula.

'Mummy, can you come and meet one of my friends tomorrow.'

'Of course,' I replied.

She suggested ten o'clock at our favourite coffee bar in Thayer Street in London's Marylebone. I suggested making it a bit later, as I had a rendezvous at nine with the dentist.

'He's leaving at midday, so he can't come later. I particularly want you to meet him, Mummy, and to tell me what you think of him.'

The dentist drilled and poked around my mouth for

what seemed like three days. On leaving his consulting rooms, face frozen solid, I found Paula waiting outside.

'Come along, Mummy. It's just around the corner.' Intrigued by her eagerness, I put a touch of lipstick on my mauve, frozen mouth, trying hard not to let a waterfall of saliva fall down my chin.

As we approached, he rose, smiled and held out his hand. The young man seemed 11 feet tall, with longish, unkempt hair and loose-fitting clothes. The handshake was firm, the smile a lazy, Scarlet Pimpernel grin. His eyes looked directly into mine and I felt as if he was reading my mind. We were served with big milky coffees, croissants and pastries, while the young man talked in a lilting, Irish accent.

At a certain moment, as I listened to his views, I forgot my frozen mouth and took a huge gulp of coffee. It went directly down my blouse and I was embarrassed. To be seen by Paula and her astonishing friend dribbling down my blouse was too much.

'Don't worry Helene, it's not important,' he said and continued his discussion. He was a thinker, a rebel against injustice and a very human young man. An hour passed like five minutes. Then, we all rose and walked towards his apartment. He said goodbye, shook hands and went inside.

Paula hurried me away to a nearby taxi rank. 'What did you think of him, Mummy?'

'He's a very remarkable young man and I liked him a lot,' I replied. Paula looked radiant, while I thought of her friend, remembering all he had said. 'He'll have a grand life that young man. I wouldn't be at all surprised if he does something unique in the world.'

Wide-eyed, Paula kissed me, opened the door of the taxi and waved before running back to the apartment. Her face was joyful. Mine was still frozen, but my brain was racing. Again, I went over everything the young man had said and thought about every detail of his face. I liked him. I've always liked him. He was, of course, Bob Geldof.

Sometime later, Paula and Bob began to live together and, as he didn't want a girlfriend who stayed in bed all day eating chocolate, she was encouraged to seek work. Finally, Paula began to write pieces for a music magazine and then for others. She had abandoned her debby accent and never talked of eating lunch at Fortnum's with her mum. It was in one of these articles that she evolved her Cinderella/Little Orphan Paula line – 'I was an abandoned child. My mother was always absent. I slept on the floor outside her room crying for her.' It was shades of Gertrude and her stories of her mother.

The proof of love is keeping quiet when falsely accused, so I kept quiet and kept my head down. Children need us when they're little and then some of them need to kill us in order to grow up. Gertrude spent her life trying to kill off my nana, but she never succeeded. Neither did Paula. Some part of her remained in the days of childhood, walking with our cats in the garden, going to the Christmas tree field so that I could fight the brambles and laughing together at so many things – like the vicar in Palma who, after twenty-five years as priest in Tangiers, surprised the congregation with 'Our Father, which art in heaven' delivered like a muezzin.

From the age of thirteen, Paula had 'crushes' every six months, year in year out, until the end of her life. She really believed that she was in love at these times, but none of them lasted and none ever would have because the only person Paula ever really loved was Bob, though she hated it when he put the brakes on her destructiveness. Unfortunately for all of us, she finally decided to kill him off, as she had me, in order to grow up. But Paula never grew up.

Often, in the still of night, I remember two dreadful moments: the last time I saw Paula and the last meeting I had with Jess about a year before his death.

Jess had sent urgent messages to me in France asking for a meeting in London. Finally, I arrived for the birthday of my granddaughter Fifi and found Jess waiting for me at Paula's house. 'I beg you, Helene, to help me. If you don't do what I ask, there will be a disaster for Paula.'

I asked what he wanted.

'I need you to travel up to Wales and get rid of the girl.'

'What girl?' I asked.

He explained. I was exasperated that he had made a drama out of his relationship with a young girl who dreamed of staying for ever. Jess cried out on leaving to take his train, 'Help me get rid of that girl. There'll be problems.'

I didn't believe him. He had always spoken with admiration of his previous girlfriend, Anita Kay. So I didn't understand – what had panicked him about the new one, the daughter of one of his former girlfriends.

The second moment was my last meeting with Paula which took place a few days before she left Bob. As I was hurrying out of the house to take the Eurostar back to France, I turned to Paula and, sure that something was wrong but not knowing what, I said, 'Try not to get too tired and don't be like your dad when he became famous and then destroyed his career and himself.'

Paula stared at me, as if shocked and walked me to the taxi. 'I'm very, very sorry, Mummy' she said, as I kissed her goodbye. I never saw her again, though I tried, many times.

She refused to see me or even to give me her address. Members of the press gave me incorrect addresses and phone numbers. When I finally reached her, she said a taxi was waiting outside and rang off. All I know is that once Bob was no longer there to guide her, Paula fell off the mountain.

She phoned me to say that she had left Bob and when I asked her if she was all right, she said she had to go and rang off. I knew nothing about Michael Hutchence. Although I went back to England to see my grand-daughters on their birthdays, I never saw Paula again. She had written these stories so often about my being an absent mother, both in articles and then in her autobiography that I think she would have found it difficult to face the reality. I didn't even know about her book. I was returning to France on Eurostar with a friend who asked me if I had read it and I said, 'Read what?'

It appeared to contain warped recollections of her time in Abergelly Chest Hospital as a child, when I drove through floods to be with her, but Paula said that I was on the other side of the Atlantic pursuing my career. It made me sound just like Joan Crawford who had put her career before her family, when, in fact, I hadn't wanted a career after I married. I had actually wanted another three children. I did try to ask her why she was doing this, but she wouldn't answer me and I resigned myself to not challenging her about it.

I only ever spoke to Michael on the phone, when I was trying to speak to Paula, who always avoided me by saying she had a taxi waiting and had to go. I think somehow she felt I had betrayed her because I had supported Bob when he went to court to get custody of the children. Michael was always pleasant to me when we spoke. When he died, I wrote to Paula, saying that she was welcome to come and stay with me in France and have the chance to rest. I knew she would be shattered by what had happened. It was such a tragedy. But, although she must have received the letter, I never had any response from her. After she moved back to London, I wrote again to arrange to see the children, but while I waited outside her house, their nanny came out and said I could only see the children outside. I didn't like the idea of them sitting on cold stone steps, so I left.

She wasn't the person I knew any more. I didn't think anything about the possibility of her using drugs. I'm not good at identifying that kind of thing anyway. When I read about Michael's drug problems, I worried about her in a general way, not because I believed that she also had an addiction. My concern was her grip on reality; she seemed not to be a part of the real world.

I had no wish to be famous, unlike Paula. Nowadays, everyone wants to be famous and Paula did things – stunts, anything – to get noticed, right to the end.

It started as a day like all the others. I fed the cats, did my shopping, drank a pot of tea in the bar and collected my post.

Later, the phone rang and a familiar voice said, 'Something terrible has happened, Helene.'

I gripped the phone wondering what had made his voice crack and I said, 'Are the children all right? Is Paula all right?'

I heard a choked back sob and then, 'She's dead, Helene.' I don't remember the next seconds. A giant block of ice seemed to have formed in my head and I stood there, trying to move and not succeeding. I kept looking at the wall and thinking, 'Paula is dead... Paula is dead.'

I heard Bob reassure me that little Tiger was safe and with her sisters and that he would call back later. I can't remember what happened next. I know I stood there, staring at the wall, unable to move, to think, to decide what I must do.

Then, suddenly, I thought of Monsieur, my second husband, who was dying at that time and I tried to think what I had to do to organise day and night nurses for him while I travelled to my child's funeral. After being in a state of suspended animation, I suddenly entered a kind of frenetic overdrive. I telephoned here and there and found an excellent nurse to take care of Monsieur in the daytime. Then, for the rest of the day, I tried to find someone for the nights. It was impossible!

In the early evening, utterly exhausted, I fell on my bed and slept until a hammering at the front door woke me. It was seven in the morning and my friend Martine Gaussens was there. She said, 'I heard about Paula's death on the radio. Have you found nurses to look after your husband?'

I said that I had someone for the days, but couldn't find anyone for the night duty. Martine immediately volunteered to come herself to do the nights. I don't know how I can ever repay this debt of friendship, but I thank her from the bottom of my heart, because she enabled me to travel to England for Paula's funeral.

First, though, I had to tell Monsieur the terrible news. For a long time he lay there, holding my hand, the tears running down his cheeks. 'I am so very sorry, Helene. For twelve years, you've had to look after me and now this tragedy. Thank God for your "military discipline". Whatever would we have done without it?'

In the evening, I realised that I had forgotten to order a wreath to be sent, so I walked upstairs to my studio and fashioned a group of flowers and leaves out of heavy card, painted them black and then gilded them in a stylised version of a Victorian funerary ornament. I took it with me to England and Bob put it on the coffin with the lilies.

The funeral that Bob organised was marvellous, different and, evidently, deeply touching, with all Paula's favourite hymns that we had so often sung together in church on Sundays. If there is a light moment at such times, at Paula's funeral it came at the end, when the pall bearers carried the coffin out to the strains of her one and only record, 'These Boots Were Made for Walking' and everyone clapped and I was happy for one brief moment that Bob had thought of such a fun way to say 'Adieu Paula'.

As I was walking through the hallway at Bob's home someone said, 'Helene, come and meet Tiger. Tiger, this is your nana.' We had never met before and we looked with great curiosity at each other. Then Tiger ran off, returning a minute later with one hand behind her back. The hand was buried in a glove puppet in the form of a crocodile that she thought might want to eat me.

I said, 'I know exactly what crocodiles like,' and began inspecting her fingers and then her feet. 'He would love to eat a few of these little pink toes.' This began a long pursuit and much laughter when the crocodile opened his mouth wide. Finally, I held her in my arms and kissed her lots of times and all the while I remembered another little girl who had loved kisses from her mum.

Tiger was the truly wonderful antidote for an anguished soul; a moment of pure, innocent joy in an unforgettably dark day.

I'm lucky I know how to live with my mountain of happy memories. I was taught when young that 'big girls don't cry'. I try not to.

EPILOGUE

What do I remember in the most vivid colours from the past?

In childhood, happiness with my grandparents: walks by the river to gather sea-pinks, breakfast at five in the morning with George in front of a wood fire and Nana's advice: 'When you're unhappy smile or you'll make everyone as unhappy as you!' I smile, Nana, I smile no matter what.

I also remember the gentleman who took me to the park and the day almost half a century later when, after discussing and describing him in detail to a Parisian friend, I returned home to Provence to show my collage pictures here in the village. There was a crowd at the opening and then, after the mayor's speech, I saw a couple enter. The lady was elegant; the gentleman smallish and walking with a stick. His hair was white, his eyes clear, his manner princely and he came straight up to me and said, 'Hello, Helene. I'm the man who knows all your secrets.'

What a moment!

I will treasure it to the end of my days, but I was so astounded, I couldn't reply. He understood and said, 'We're looking forward to seeing your pictures. Do explain them.' And I walked at his side, trying to explain my visual ideas. He paused in front of one that represented summer in a grouping of the four seasons. 'Ah, those are "Les roses d'Hélène de Ronsard".' And he recited the poem, as he had all those years before.

'He loves poetry,' said his wife and I replied, 'I do, too.'

He liked best my mathematic 'tweeds' based on the Irish woven material, which is very difficult to recreate in collage. Only collectors buy those. He chose one in Bordeaux red and gold. Then he invited me to his summer home and we met often, like old friends. He was a remarkable gentleman and I hope my suspicions were right. I shall never know, of course, but I adored him for fifty years. He died two years after our meeting at the exhibition at a very old age.

Of Jess, I remember his wildest fantasies and the rise in his blood pressure when I played the women roles of which he dreamed. I remember his almost comic cowardice, his malapropisms and his desire to sing like Sinatra when his voice was pure Vera Lynn. I remember, too, his violence and his frustration with himself. Like Paula, despite his great talent, Jess was a wannabe. The problem was that he wanted to be someone he could never be. Paula wanted to be me until the age of sixteen and then a 6-foot tall Jerry Hall with long red hair, not 5 feet 2 inches with hair bleached to near baldness. Jess wanted to be the legendary bon viveur and Don-Juan-like figure Porfirio Rubirosa, or Al Capone, or Paul Newman. It rendered him speechless with rage when I said, once, 'I just want to be me, if you'll allow me to be me.'

I remember leaving the house on the hill and the exquisite silence of Snowdonia and embarking with Paula on a long voyage to the sun in our van, nicknamed Fanta Fiat. We were so happy at last to live in the golden South.

Of the wild years, when I felt liberated from my marriage and much more my own person, I remember men of all shapes and sizes in hot pursuit, shouting out compliments in Piccadilly, or suggesting very odd pursuits. I remember Fellini screeching with fright and Visconti's elegance. I've tried all my life to follow his advice – 'Write about your life, Elena. You're not like other people. You don't react or think like others, but they will like sharing your life' – and here I am, at last, doing just that.

In that same period, I remember travelling to all manner of strange and remote places that I put in my novels but not in this book. A book in the future perhaps! I'm glad I went to the desert of Central Asia and the Caucasus when I did. I was young and brave and strong and the world had not been putrefied to the extent it now has with such violence and hate that murder has become a mundane occurrence and drug-induced lunacy is commonplace. I wouldn't be able to go to all those places now. Everything has its time and in my old age, I can enjoy Provence – its vines, its golden light and my brigade of peace-loving cats. I remember Sicily and the aftermath of my visit and deciding, at last, to write. It took me many years to learn but I was published while learning and I hope, in all humility, to improve as the years go by.

Of Paula, I remember the happiness, the laughter and the sadness. If Paula hurt a lot of people, and she did, it's partly my fault for not having realised that even small children can need a psychiatrist. There are no excuses. In the sixties, young women like me didn't know a great deal about psychology and behavioural problems. Now they do, but I'm not sure that it always makes life better. And one can't help but wonder if a psychiatrist would have made a difference in Paula's case and would have helped to explain all the strange things that she did. I think of her often and my memorial to her is in my head.

I could have described the Paula–Bob household, as many of their so-called friends have done, but I believe that the family scenes, wonderful as they were, belong to them. What I will say is that Bob has always been marvellous to me and always given me a great welcome whenever I have visited him and my granddaughters. We don't discuss sad things, we all talk, usually at the same time.

I started out to write this book for my grandchildren and for Bob. I didn't realise that the deep pool of memories would be so traumatic. It's been like undergoing psychotherapy by creation. One moment I was reliving a fierce row during my childhood and the next I was lying on my back in an allotment looking up at the sky and listening to the bees buzzing round my head. Or I would recall polishing brasses, or the perfume from a vase of flowers and tinkering around with my father's clocks.

And what now? I'm growing old in my own way, wrinkled like a prune by the sun, un-lifted, un-Botoxed and hoping to look like Georgia O'Keefe in her Santa Fe period, if I live long enough. Wish me luck!

From this French village, surrounded by the vines of Provence, to all my readers, a hand outstretched to say hello and thank you for buying my books.